AF247570

"These are human beings. I see them as my children."
—Anna Rodriguez

Ma'am Anna

The Anna Rodriguez Story
The Remarkable Story of a Human Trafficking Rescuer

Anna Rodriguez
as told to Anthony Bunko

Ma'am Anna

The Anna Rodriguez Story
The Remarkable Story of a Human Trafficking Rescuer

TitleTown Publishing, LLC
P.O. Box 12093 Green Bay, WI 54307-12093
920.737.8051 | titletownpublishing.com

Editorial Consultant: Mike Josephson
Editor: Amanda Bindel
Cover Design: Janice Rossi
Intrior Design: Erika L. Block

PUBLISHER'S CATALOGING-IN-PUBLICATION DATA:

Rodriguez, Anna, 1957-
Ma'am Anna, the Anna Rodriguez story : the remarkable story of a human trafficking rescuer / Anna Rodriguez as told to Anthony Bunko. -- Green Bay, WI : TitleTown Publishing, c2013.

p. ; cm.
ISBN: 978-0-9888605-4-4

Summary: Human trafficking has infiltrated not only the international community but the United States. Ma'am Anna is a modern-day abolitionist and hero. Her memoir puts the reader inside human trafficking and chronicles how one woman dared to track and hunt traffickers and recover stolen people being sold as property. Her story shows that one courageous person really can make a difference. Survivor updates are included.--Publisher.

1. Rodriguez, Anna, 1957- 2. Human trafficking--United States. 3. Child trafficking--United States. 4. Abduction--United States. 5. Human trafficking--United States--Prevention. 6. Abduction--United States--Prevention. 7. Human trafficking victims--United States--Personal narratives. I. Bunko, Anthony. II. Title. III. Title: The Anna Rodriguez story.

HQ281 .R63 2013
306.3/620973--dc23   1303

*(Names and some details throughout this book
have been changed to protect the innocent.)*

Ma'am Anna

The Anna Rodriguez Story
The Remarkable Story of a Human Trafficking Rescuer

Anna Rodriguez
as told to Anthony Bunko

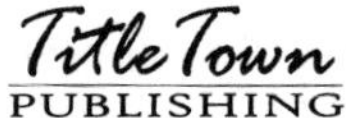

TitleTown
PUBLISHING

The Ricky Martin Foundation is very grateful to Anna Rodriguez's commitment to end human trafficking. Anna's activism and knowledge regarding the second most lucrative crime in the world has undoubtedly strengthened our mission to educate and protect children and youth against this atrocity as well as safeguard their human rights.

—Ricky Martin, singer/performer

I would like dedicate this book to my family, friends, colleagues, supporters and, most of all, the victims and survivors of human trafficking around the world. I would also like to dedicate this book and the work I do to my son, Jose Gabriel, who passed away at the age of forty-three days due to a heart condition. He is my inspiration and my guardian angel who guides and protects me every single day. I love you and miss you!

Peace, love, freedom and faith are the four most important words in the universe.

—Anna Rodriguez

I dedicate this book to my parents who have always been there for me whenever I needed them. Also to the remarkable Anna who has given me such an insight into the terrible injustice which exists in the world today and the bravery and struggle some people face in their daily lives to overcome it. Stay free.

—Anthony Bunko

Contents

Summertime Guatemala 1998

With her knees tucked up to her chin, nineteen-year-old Chica Garcia sat on a thin mattress on the dirt floor of her small kitchen. Next to her, wrapped in an old tattered blanket, her twenty-day-old baby girl lay fast asleep. The newborn had been ill with a fever for a few days and her constant crying made it a trying time for everyone in the household. It was so hot and humid Chica moved her modest bed and the sick infant from the bedroom she shared with her six brothers and one sister to the kitchen because it was the coolest place in the house, and even then it was unbearably hot.

However, it wasn't just her baby's illness the teenager was worried about. Through the gap in the kitchen door, by the light of several candles, she could see her father slumped in a chair in the adjacent living room while Jose Tecum paced around, flailing his arms about. The shadow of his short, thick frame bounced off the walls.

They were both drinking, heavily.

"I want her. I'm going to marry her," Tecum's voice echoed around the room.

Chica's father didn't reply. He sat there silent, not daring to speak or even look Tecum in the eye.

The short, middle-aged guest was a powerful man in Patachaj, a small rural village in Guatemala. He belonged to an influential family; his brother was the mayor who ruled the small, police-less village with fear. Jose was a coyote. By smuggling people across borders, he made a great deal of money. The brothers took what they wanted when they wanted it and were ruthless to those that resisted.

"I want you to hand her over to me," Tecum spoke again. "I will look after her."

Chica's skin crawled at the sound of his deep voice. If her baby weren't so ill, she would have run away and hid until the monster had gone.

"N…n…no," her father slurred his words as he finally spoke to the man in front of him. "She doesn't wa… wa…. want to go with you."

She cradled the baby in her arms, rocking back and forth trying her best to drown out the heated conversation coming from the next room by quietly singing a lullaby to the infant. The little one was burning up.

Tecum poured more liquor into Chica's father's glass. He sat down, changing his approach. His voice softer, "I've already had her, you know. If you don't let her come with me and she gets pregnant again I won't help her or you."

Tears rolled down Chica's cheeks as she remembered the day he followed her to the market. It was a Wednesday afternoon. She hadn't noticed him at first, but she knew he would be there somewhere, watching her, waiting to talk to her. He'd been stalking and harassing her for months. On that day he appeared by her side as she bought some fruit for the family dinner. "Chica," he muttered, "can I walk with you?"

She ignored him, took her bag and carried on through the crowded streets.

"Chica… but I love you," he followed after her.

She shrugged him off.

"I want you, Chica."

She raced back to her house; he followed closely behind. When she got there, no one was home. Her baby was with her mother; her father was out working; and her brothers and sister were at school. Without asking permission, Tecum followed her inside.

"Go away!" She tried to push him out. He grabbed her and dragged her into a bedroom.

"No." She kicked and thrashed struggling to pull free. "Please just go away," she begged, but it was no use. He was too strong and too determined. He pushed her onto the bed and forced himself upon her. She tried to scream, but he covered her mouth with his hand. He raped her right there on her parent's bed. As soon as it was over, he left and, strangely, took her shoes and a hair clip with him.

The sound of a glass smashing against the wall brought Chica back to the present and the conversation in the other room; more raised voices, more liquor. She prayed he would just leave. He made her skin crawl.

As much as the noise of the commotion bothered her; the silence frightened her more. The hush meant her father had passed out from the whiskey Jose Tecum had brought with him and insisted they drink. Chica's father couldn't resist a drink. Tecum played on it. She knew Tecum would come to her and rape her again. It had gone on since the day he had followed her home—he appeared every few days, demanding Chica leave with him, threatening her parents, getting her father drunk and then forcing himself on her.

In the next room, Tecum's tone was getting more aggressive. He hissed, spitting his demands. Her father didn't say much in return. "Hand her over to me or I'll kill her and I'll kill you. Do you hear me? I will kill you both! At any moment I will take her away!" Her father got scared. He gave Chica to him. There was nobody there to help Chica and her family.

Again silence. Chica's father got to his feet and trudged outside. Tecum followed close behind.

Chica tried her best to stay awake, but eventually exhaustion took over. She drifted off to sleep. A while later she was forcefully awoken. Tecum stood above her, lust etched on his face. She had no idea where her father had gone. Tecum undid his trousers. She struggled, but again she was powerless to resist. He grabbed her wrists firmly, ripped her nightgown off her shoulders and climbed on top of her. His whiskey breath covered her face as he plunged deep inside her. Chica stared across at her little girl, who luckily was sleeping peacefully. Chica closed her eyes feeling hatred and loathing as Tecum tried to kiss her.

He didn't take long. His sweat dripped onto her skin. "I love you, Chica," he muttered, getting to his feet and pulling his trousers up.

She turned away from him, covering herself up.

He grabbed her firmly by the arm. "Up... come on... you're coming with me!"

Chica looked up at him, confused. He had never actually tried to take her before.

"I said get up. It's all agreed with your father. Now hurry."

"No. I'm not," she argued with him. "I don't love you."

Jose Tecum ignored her indignant pleas and pulled her roughly up by the hair, dragging her to her feet. "I said come on. If you don't, I will kill you!"

Chica didn't want to go with him but he forced her, she didn't have a choice.

She wanted to wake her family to come to her rescue, but she was scared. She didn't want anything to happen to them. She hurriedly put on a coat and her shoes and took her baby and went with him.

Chica put her baby in Tecum's car and sat down in the passenger seat. He started the car; she scooped up the baby and cradled her tightly as the car drove off into the night.

For two long months, Chica lived a life of imprisonment in Tecum's large house on the outskirts of the village. His home mirrored his powerful status in the village. It resembled a fortress, surrounded by large fences, an acre or so of land and a huge gate that was always locked, not just to keep intruders out but to keep Chica in. With no police in the village, she, or her family, could not get anyone to help them.

Chica stayed there alone with her baby, not allowed to venture out, not allowed to meet or talk to anyone. If she threatened to run away, her abductor promised he would not only find her and drag her back, but he would kill her family.

Scared and lonely, Chica spent her time doing chores around the house for no pay, and most nights he forced her to have sex with him against her will.

Then one night her little girl got sick again. This time the baby's stomach swelled up twice the normal size, but Tecum refused to let Chica take the baby to the doctor. Chica did not have any money to pay a doctor, and Tecum would not give her any money either.

Throughout the night the baby's condition got worse; she wailed uncontrollably. Tecum got angry; he drank whiskey and yelled at Chica to shut the child up. Chica held the little girl in her arms, trying to sing her to sleep. When the screaming was more than he could stand, Tecum finally called a doctor but it was too late—the poor baby died in Chica's arms. On Tecum's instructions, the doctor took the baby away. Chica never saw her little girl again.

At first Chica refused to accept the loss of the infant. She wandered around the house in a daze, thinking she could hear her little baby crying in the next room. When reality set in, depression soon took hold of her. She cried herself to sleep at night and in the day retreated even further into her lonely shell. She stopped eating. She longed even more to see her family, but Tecum would not allow it. In her darkest hours, she considered ending her life. As cold as ice, Tecum carried on as if nothing had happened. He continued to force Chica to have intercourse with him almost every night.

One night after dinner, as she sat in her room, he barged in. "Hurry up. We're going out."

Chica was shocked. He had never taken her anywhere before. "Where are we going?" she asked.

"A small village called Polouac. It's up in the mountains. There's a festival there, and I want you to meet someone. Now hurry." He stormed out and waited for her in his car.

Hesitantly she changed her clothes. She'd heard rumors of Polouac being a place of witchcraft and a place where evil things went on. Reluctantly she climbed into his car.

The journey took ages as they travelled high up into the mountains on small dangerous roads. Tecum drove fast and hardly said a word the entire time; he just kept looking across at her and smirking. It was dark by the time they arrived at the small village. Huts surrounded a circle of fire with bright flames of different colors. Dead animals hung on poles; people danced around chanting to the sound of manic drumming.

"What are we doing here?"

"You'll see. Now get out," he said gesturing towards her door.

Tecum came around to her side and grabbed Chica by the arm, dragging her to a hut surrounded by a small crowd of people.

An elderly woman grabbed the back of her head and forced a drink down her throat. The chanting got louder, the drumming faster. Suddenly a wild-looking man with a bare chest appeared from out of a hut. He was tall, his face and body covered in white and red paint. His glazed eyes didn't seem to blink at all, just glared at everyone in turn; a long snake wrapped itself around his shoulders.

"Now you are going to love me," Tecum whispered into Chica's ear and squeezed her hand.

Chica sat still, afraid to move. Her head started spinning and her vision became hazy. She tried to get to her feet, but her legs refused to work. She felt dizzy. The woman grabbed her shoulders and pushed her back to the ground. The wild looking man, she assumed must have been one of the witch doctors she had only heard rumors about, danced above her, sprinkling dust all over her skin. He chanted in a deep voice. Tecum stood back, a wicked grin on his face.

"What's going on?" Chica turned to face Tecum. That was the last thing she recalled as she blacked out.

A while later she woke up on the ground feeling very groggy.

"Let's get you back to the car and back home." Tecum helped her to her feet.

"What happened? I feel strange."

He didn't reply. He drove back down the mountainside toward their village.

"I don't remember a thing," Chica mentioned.

"Don't worry. The witch doctor made everything right," he muttered. "You will love me now, forever."

"What?"

He stopped the car and stared at her for a few seconds. "He put a spell on you so you will love me."

"I will never love you," Chica bravely spat out her words.

"You don't understand. If you don't love me, some terrible fate will be unleashed on you and your family." He started laughing. "The witch doctor used a lock of your hair and your shoes to cast his spell and now I have full control over your soul and your spirit." Tecum showed her a lock of her own hair that he put carefully into a pocket in his wallet.

As far as Chica was concerned, nothing changed. She still despised him more than ever, but she was petrified, fearing for the safety of her family.

A week or so later, he told her they were going away again. They left in the middle of the night, this time in Tecum's brother Juan's car. Juan drove them. Jose Tecum sat in the front seat, speaking quietly with Juan. He refused to tell her where they were going. Juan dropped them off in Quetzaltenango.

After riding on the bus a long time, the driver dropped them off at the edge of the desert. They started walking. Chica had no clothes and nothing else to her name. There was very little food, and what they did have Tecum ate most of himself, leaving her only a few scraps now and then. She had to drink water from streams while he had his own fresh supply. They walked for days. She had no idea how many. She was exhausted and drained from travelling in the hot sun and trying to keep warm on the cold nights. Her feet were blistered and her skin dry.

One night, under the cover of darkness, instead of resting, they crossed a river.

"Where are we?" she asked.

"Mexico. In a few hundred yards we will be in America." He held her hand to help her wade across. They crossed into the United States, and the first place they went was Eloy, Arizona.

Chica had always wanted to go to America, but the America she found herself in was a million miles away from what she had heard about.

Tecum met a man in a bar. They shook hands. Next thing, she found herself sleeping next to her abductor in a cramped section of flooring in a smelly back room in a rundown house. They house was crammed with other illegal immigrants who had also snuck across the border.

During the day, they worked in fields in California, picking grapes to pay for room and board. She longed to go home, escape from this life and head back to Guatemala. But she was lost in this vast new country without anyone to turn to.

They worked there for fifteen days before he again informed her they were moving on.

"We are going somewhere else now," he told her.

"I don't want to go anywhere else. I want to go back home," Chica said, bravely, as they took a bus across the country, "back to my parents."

He laughed. "You can… after you pay me back the 8,000 quetzales (about $2,000 US dollars) you owe me for bringing you to America."

She sat there, stunned by his words. "But I didn't want to come here."

He dismissed her reply. "We're going to Florida, a town called Immokalee." He grabbed her arm and looked into her face. "And when we get there, when you meet my wife, you will have to tell her you are my son's wife. Do you understand?'

"Your wife?"

"You heard me," he spat his words at her. "Just do as I say. Otherwise I'll kill you and your family." Tecum and Chica rode on a bus to Florida. Chica noticed that there was an ugly, skinny dog on the back of the bus.

Once they arrived in Florida, Tecum's wife stared suspiciously at her husband and Chica as they walked into the small apartment. She looked the girl up and down.

"Who's she?" she asked Tecum.

He took his wife into the next room. Chica looked around the small, cramped second floor apartment. To her surprise, not only was he married but he had two sons and a daughter.

When the wife appeared, she still wasn't happy, and she stormed into the kitchen. The first week was awkward. The wife questioned her endlessly, but Tecum was never far from the pair. Chica slept on a small thin mattress on the floor in the same bedroom as Tecum and his wife. He kept looking at her, trying to touch her when his wife fell asleep.

During the day, she picked peppers, pumpkins and tomatoes with other workers in the vast fields in the region. Tecum always worked with her, side by side. He told her to tell people she was his niece and was only fifteen-years-old in case investigators questioned her. He destroyed all of her identification documents and demanded she sign her paychecks over to him to pay off her debt.

Chica wasn't allowed to talk to anyone. She had no friends, and she was not permitted to leave the tiny apartment unless she was working. While Tecum's wife was out working every evening, Chica did chores around the house.

Her life was a misery, a living hell. Left with no money, exhausted from all the work, she was violated sexually when Tecum's wife was out. He frightened her into silence by telling her to remember the spell and if she told anyone then something bad was going to happen. She began to lose the will to live. A field slave in the day, a sex slave at night.

After six long months of living in America, Chica found herself in a vicious circle in which she had no escape until the night Mrs. Tecum came home unexpectedly and caught her husband in bed with her.-

The wife dragged Chica by the hair, screaming and yelling. Tecum exploded, beating his wife up. Someone must have called 9-1-1. The police stormed in and arrested Tecum. Chica's life was about to change. And so was mine.

The Lock of Hair

I sat alone in my car staring up at the two-story apartment building from across the street on a hot Florida day in 1999. The words I read in the police report still echoed in my head.

"Something doesn't add up here," it stated. *"The girl caught in bed by the wife would not respond to questioning. Don't think she wanted to be there. She was crying and very despondent."*

Apart from the overgrown landscape, the Mediterranean yellow building was well maintained, unlike most of the run-down dormitory style housing I was used to visiting in town.

I flipped through the report one more time making sure I hadn't missed any details. The incident, which had taken place the night before, didn't read much differently than the other domestic violence cases I'd been involved in. *Wife comes home early, catches husband in bed with another woman, all hell breaks loose, police called, man arrested on a battery charge and domestic violence and now in jail.*

Apparently the poor wife had been beaten up quite badly and was extremely distressed by the time the police arrived. However, that wasn't the reason I put all my other cases to the side and skipped my morning soda. It was that handwritten note the arresting officer had left on top of the file that intrigued me. *Something doesn't add up here.*

Deputy Sheriff Roman, the arresting officer was a well-respected officer on the Collier County sheriff's department. I had known him for several years, and I knew if Deputy Sheriff Roman felt something was wrong, then something was wrong. Putting the police report away, I grabbed my hand-held radio and stepped out of my car. Just past nine in the morning and already baking hot.

Immokalee, Florida, is only about forty-five minutes from where I live in the town of Naples. But the two places couldn't be any more different. Naples, with its art galleries, expensive shops and boutiques is commonly known as the Beverly Hills of Southwest Florida. The wealthy dine at five-star restaurants and sun themselves on the white sands. Immokalee, on the other hand, is a small quiet agricultural town with a few small Mexican taco places and mom and pop diners. The mostly Spanish-speaking population spends long hours for very little pay picking vegetables from the acres of farmland. Tomatoes, cucumbers, bell peppers, potatoes, citrus and other fresh items harvested in the blazing sun every day are shipped all over the country.

I knew the place well and several of the residents knew me. In my role, I often dealt with cases of sexual abuse, domestic violence, and death notifications among other call outs in and around the Collier Country in Florida.

***

Being from Puerto Rico, I could easily relate to the Spanish-speaking community. When I first started working as a victim advocate for the Collier County Sheriff's Office, the immigrants didn't seem to trust the law enforcement or anyone who worked with them. I made it a priority to break the fear the migrants had towards the authorities.

After a lot of thinking and soul searching, I developed a "home visitation" program. If I knew where the people lived, I would go to their homes and meet with them. This made for long workdays to allow me to meet with victims and witnesses after they came back from work. Some days, I started the morning shift late so I could work into the evening, until nine or ten o'clock at night. Other days, I would go to the bus stops at five in the morning looking for the people on their way to work.

I had my files and would ask people, "Where is Pedro Such and Such or Lupe What's Her Name?"

"Oh that's him or that's her."

And I would approach them.

Many times I'd call home to let my family know I would not make it for supper. It was inconvenient at the time for my husband and three children, but it was well worth all the effort to gain the trust of the community.

The program proved such a success that a couple of months later when I would arrive at the office, lines of people would be waiting to speak with me. The lobby looked more like a doctor's office than a police station. Instead of having to go out looking for people, they were coming to me. The detectives in the area were pleased because instead of suspending cases, they were able to move the cases forward since they now had victim and witness statements.

The citizens of Immokalee spread the word about the woman at the police station who helps people. People within the migrant community knew that if they had a problem they could call me. I was proud that the local immigrants trusted me.

So I adjusted my schedule to allow for non-traditional hours.

Making my way across the parking lot, I tried to ignore the sharp pains shooting through my lower back. The pain had been getting worse and a lot more frequent over the past few weeks. My husband kept telling me quite strongly to get it checked out. But I was much too busy to find time to get it sorted out; I had lots of work to do. I was not a fan of going to the doctor's office. I hate needles. I had a feeling it might be something serious, but I just didn't want to deal with it now.

Two young boys, probably in their early twenties, looked up at me from under the hood of a beat up Chevy. I guess my blond hair made me look out of place in the town of mostly dark-haired Hispanic women. Their eyes followed me as I walked past them and toward the entrance of the apartment building.

Slightly out of breath, I reached the second floor. My heart beat fast in my chest. Feeling a little uneasy, I tried to focus on what I was going to say. I tapped gently on the door, trying not to make it sound too official and threatening.

I waited.

The blare from a television set drifted across the hallway from the next apartment.

Before I could knock again, the door shot open a few inches with a sharp violent jerk. I stepped back in surprise. A woman's face peered out at me, clearly Hispanic with her light brown skin and almost black eyes. She was small, smaller than I am, and I'm only five foot two! Her right cheek appeared to be bruised and slightly swollen.

Clearly still upset, she turned to yell at someone inside before looking me up and down suspiciously. Her eyes stopped to briefly look at the small sheriff's logo on my T-shirt. I always made a point to dress down when on duty; jeans, T-shirt and white tennis shoes were my standard uniform. In my mind it was less intimidating and it helped to lower the *them* verses *us* barrier. The logo on my shirt was the only indication that I had anything to do with the authorities.

"Hello, Mrs. Tecum. I'm Anna," I said in Spanish, and smiled softly. Her expression didn't change. She just glared. "Look, I'm not a police officer," I added, "I'm just here to make sure you're okay."

She continued to eye me up and down before closing the door in my face. I stood there alone again, wondering what to do next. Then the door opened again—just enough for her to squeeze out without giving me the chance to see anything inside. I tried not to stare at the bruises on her arms. They looked painful.

"I don't need help!" she protested. "I'm fine. Please just go away."

"Mrs. Tecum," I pleaded. "Your husband may be home soon. I wanted to see if you needed any help and to explain the legal process to you."

She hesitated for several seconds before apprehensively opening the door and letting me pass.

The heat hit me as soon as I walked in. The apartment must have been well over ninety degrees inside. The room had a central air-conditioning unit but it must have been switched off or broken. Then the stench of sweat overtook me. It was almost unbearable.

Glancing around the sparsely furnished apartment, I noticed three young children, two boys and a girl, barely clothed, sitting on the floor in the kitchen near a wooden table eating white rice out of a large bowl with their hands. Behind them a stack of dirty pots and dishes filled the sink. There were pots on the stove with dried up food still inside.

In the room where I stood was an old style TV set pushed in one corner. There was no other furniture except a twin size bed shoved up against the wall near the window.

Perched on the edge of the bed was a young girl. She didn't look much older than sixteen. I assumed she was the girl mentioned in the note from Deputy Sheriff Roman.

Her head was bowed, and her long scraggily hair hung down covering her face; her hands were clasped in her lap. She wasn't dressed like a typical teenager. Instead of jeans or sweat pants, she wore a long woven native dress. Although rather shabby looking, it was strikingly colorful with a mix of whites, reds and blues.

"Where's my husband? When will he be home?" The wife's demanding questions snapped me out of my trance.

"He's still in jail," I replied. "He will need to pay a bond to get out." My words made her even more irate. She paced about back and forth, arms flailing. "It's her fault! It's her fault!" She pointed at the young girl. "It's because of her my husband's in jail. They didn't go to work today. Look at my kids, nothing to eat, only rice…no food." She rambled on angrily.

I glanced from the irate woman to the young girl. She still hadn't moved a muscle despite all the hatred directed her way. I turned back.

"Can I get you some food for you and your children?" I said, hoping it would calm the woman down.

"No!" she indignantly replied, "My husband will get us food when he gets back. He will care for his family."

"Who is she?" I couldn't resist myself, nodding towards the bed.

"She is my husband's son's wife." She hissed impatiently.

"Oh, your husband has an older son?" I asked, not meaning for it to be a trick question.

She shook her head violently. 'No…no…no…these are my husband's only children." She pointed to the three young children still sitting on the floor.

"Who is she then?" I asked now thoroughly confused. Her conflicting story gave me more reason to believe something was definitely wrong.

"I don't know," she finally confessed. "I don't know who she is.

"I need to speak to her alone," I said, something didn't add up, and I needed to figure it out.

"No!" the wife yelled at me, obviously flustered and extremely annoyed.

"Mrs. Tecum," I took control, "If you don't settle down and let me talk to this young lady, I will have to call for backup. I am here to help." I reached for my radio.

She huffed loudly. "I don't care! Talk to her!" She stormed off into the kitchen.

I turned back to the girl. "Hola," I said softly, kneeling down so I could look up at her. I wanted her to feel comfortable so I moved down to her eye level. "What is your name?" I spoke very slowly in very basic and elementary Spanish.

The features of her face were sunken and drawn. Her beautiful dark brown eyes looked red and swollen with dark circles underneath.

"Chica." She said, finally glancing up at me, her voice so quiet I could barely hear her.

"Come with me Chica? Outside… I just want to talk to you, just outside the door, only for a minute." From the kitchen the sound of dishes clanging and pots banging broke the silence. Chica nodded her head. I took her hand. It felt so frail and delicate, as though it might break in mine if I squeezed too hard. I led her out into the hallway. I closed the door behind us.

Nervously she peered back at the apartment door as we sat down on the top step. I brought her outside so she would not be intimidated by Mrs. Tecum. We sat down. Again I wanted to speak with her eye to eye. Let her know that we were two equals. I was not talking down to her. I was there as her friend. I was there to help her. Again I used very simple Spanish words so Chica could understand. So she would be at ease.

"How old are you?" I asked.

"Fifteen."

"Oh my God!" I said in shock. "Why aren't you in school?"

"He doesn't let me go to school," Chica said. "All he does is have me work in the tomato fields, picking tomatoes. I work all day. And he doesn't even give me twenty-five cents to buy a Coca-Cola!"

"You don't get paid for the work?"

"No, he takes all the money," she explained.

Her head hung limply. Off in the distance the siren of a police car wailed loudly then drifted off into the distance. Her body tensed, but she still refused to look up. I gently rubbed her shoulder, letting the silence comfort her.

"What's wrong Chica? Please tell me. I can help."

Without looking up, she finally whispered, "El me trata como un esclava!" *He treats me like a slave!*

"What?" her words refused to sink into my brain.

"I feel like a slave. All I do is work, work, work, and he won't even give me money to buy a Coca-Cola." She said that at least three times. She looked at me. "He takes all my money, and then he makes me sleep with him while his wife is working at night."

I sat stunned as she went on to tell me her story of how she had ended up in the United States.

I let her do all the talking, holding her hand in comfort. Once she started, it was as if an emotional dam had burst inside her. Crying, she told me how the husband, Jose Tecum, had gotten her father drunk back in her village in Guatemala and when he fell asleep he had taken her and her baby away.

"Where's your baby now, Chica?"

Her grip on my hand tightened. "She died. She got ill, and he wouldn't let me take her to see a doctor."

My heart sank. Tears welled in my eyes and then ran down my cheeks as the memory of the baby I lost came flooding back to me. Even today I can still picture his delicate little face as he peacefully passed away in my arms. He was only forty-three days old in May of 1982, three days after Mother's Day. And although I knew he wasn't well, born with a heart condition, and I knew he probably wouldn't make it, it devastated my husband and me. I still think of him every day; he's always with me.

It was the saddest day of my life. The nurse had to pry him from my arms. His name was Jose Gabriel, and he is still my angel, my little angel up there in heaven.

I see my son in every child victim I rescue; maybe it was that one dreadful moment in our lives that became the reason I want to save as many children as I can.

I looked at Chica. I could feel the same emptiness I had felt in her voice. I knew I had to get her out of there as fast as I could. The sense of urgency inside of me kicked in. I asked her if she was related to Jose. She said: "No."

"You like Coca-Cola, Chica?" I asked, trying my best to hide the panic in my voice. "I can get you a Coke. Come on." I urged.

"No!" she responded weakly. "I can't. I shouldn't have told you anything. I need to go back in now!"

"It's okay, Chica," I gently put my hand on her shoulders to tried to keep her from rising up off the step.

"No...I can't," she repeated. "He will kill me. My family will die...I can't leave...I can't leave... He put a spell... brujo... brujo." The fear on her face was evident, her body almost shaking.

"Chica… he can't hurt you… he has no spell on you!"

"He can…he has a lock of my hair… he took me to witch doctor and he put witchcraft on it… he has power… if I don't do what he tells me he will hurt me and my family."

She squeezed my hand tightly. I took a deep breath, trying to compose myself. Just at that moment, the door opened and the wife stood there, arms folded. Chica released her grip on my hand and darted past her into the apartment. I looked back at the wife; she glared at me for a second, hatred etched on her features.

She slammed the door shut.

I sat there helpless for several moments. My head spun as I headed back to my car.

Brujo.

I hadn't heard that word in a long time. It's Spanish for witchcraft and many of the rural Hispanic communities still believed in it. Back in Puerto Rico when I was growing up, witch doctors were well respected and feared in the country. I had friends who went to see them to put curses on their enemies or more often than not to put love spells on those they secretly admired. I'd even heard quite repulsive stories about witch doctors using the brains of dead babies or menstrual blood to make their spells stronger. So I knew that, to Chica, the threat was very real. Witchcraft and slavery, two ancient and uncivilized concepts I never thought I would encounter.

With no idea what to do next, I headed back to my office. I couldn't get the girl out of my mind. My stomach was tied up in too many knots to eat. I picked up the other cases stacked on my desk, but I couldn't concentrate on anything but that poor girl trapped in the apartment. I just kept worrying about Chica. Thoughts of her consumed me. I didn't want to imagine what would happen to her if she were still home when the tyrant that raped her every night came home.

Deputy Sheriff Roman was back on duty, and I filled him in about the situation, trying to contain my emotions.

"Anna, call me if you need any help," he told me and he headed off on his rounds.

"Thanks," I said.

I drove around the block, head spinning. I returned to the apartment again and again and again. Each time Mrs. Tecum got more and more irritated. At one point I thought she was going to hit me. The threat of me calling for back up got me inside the apartment. But each time, no matter what I said, Chica would not leave, still terrified her family would suffer in some way.

Back in my office, I got the call from the jail alerting me. Jose Tecum had posted bail. Panic engulfed me. A massive wave of adrenaline washed over me. Suddenly, I had a plan of attack. Rushing to my desk, I called my friend Donna, a supervisor and respected contact at the Department of Children and Family Services.

"Answer, please answer." I prayed and glanced at my watch as the phone rang. Nothing. I hung up. Within five seconds, I dialed again.

This was a race against time with every second feeling like a minute, every minute like an hour. Finally Donna picked up.

"Donna, it's me, Anna," I blurted out. "I need your help." I managed to stay calm as I told her everything. When I finished there was silence on the other end.

"Anna," she finally broke the silence. "I don't think I can do anything really unless you're sure she's under eighteen and a relative of the family."

"Please," I pleaded; I didn't want my only hope to be blocked by red tape. "Donna, "I begged, "If we don't get her out, I'm afraid of what might happen to her. Please! She's just a child... a scared and lonely child!"

Another long pause as Donna contemplated what I had just told her.

"Okay, Anna, fax me a request quickly." I heaved a silent sigh of relief. "In the meantime, I'll send an investigator to meet you at your office immediately... Now, I want you to write the request exactly like this...."

I feverishly scribbled down the information exactly as she told me and faxed it over with trembling hands. The clock above the door screamed out it was almost five o'clock. I prayed the traffic from the jail was as bad as it normally was. That would at least give me an extra fifteen minutes or so to help Chica.

The female Department of Children and Families investigator finally pulled up. It felt like an eternity waiting but was actually only fifteen minutes. I raced down the steps to meet her, calling Deputy Sheriff Roman for some back-up on the radio as I went. I didn't want to contemplate if I was too late for the girl. Thank God the apartment was nearby. Deputy Sheriff Roman was already there, standing outside his patrol car when we pulled up.

I rushed up the stairs; the DCF investigator and Deputy Sheriff Roman close behind, the adrenaline surging through my veins. "Let me do the talking," I said to the investigator as we neared the apartment. "We don't want to upset the wife or scare the poor girl any more than she already is."

"I'll wait outside the door in case the husband comes back," reassured Deputy Sheriff Roman.

I banged on the door.

No answer.

"Mrs. Tecum let me in." I banged loudly. "Mrs. Tecum… if you don't let me in, I will get the police to force the door open."

Slowly it opened up. An angry and nervous Mrs. Tecum blocked my path. I walked passed her. "Chica," I shouted.

The girl appeared from the bedroom, her eyes swollen from crying, her body shaking. "I'm here to take you out of here." I glared back at the wife.

"No… no… I can't go… my family… the spell..." Chica hesitated backing up against the wall.

I don't know where my next sentence came from. It wasn't planned; I just said the first thing that sprung into my head. "I've just come from a witch doctor in Immokalee, Chica… and he's broken the spell… you're free… you're free to come with me."

The investigator stared at me, not knowing what was going on.

Chica just stood there, and then a smile lit up her face. It was beautiful. She looked as if a giant weight had been lifted off her shoulders. "Yes," she said softly, "I will come."

I grinned back at her, tears welling up in my eyes. The relief felt incredible, washing over me like a tidal wave of emotion. I just wanted to run over and hug her, but I knew we didn't have time. A car door slamming outside reminded me of the urgency of the situation. "Let's get your stuff," I hurried her.

"No! She owes us money! She can't go!" the wife screamed.

Ignoring her protests, I followed Chica into the bedroom, Mrs. Tecum in tow still frantically yelling. My mouth dropped open as I walked inside and saw the sleeping quarters. There were two mattresses and a small mat on the crowded floor. The room was a mess, clothes everywhere. I knew right away which spot was Chica's.

She picked up a small bag next to the mat, placed a shirt, two pairs of panties and a bra inside. That's all she had to her name except for what she was wearing.

I picked up a small pair of jeans lying on the floor next to the mat. "Are they yours," I said, holding them up. They were caked in dirt and tomato stains.

She frowned. "Yes… but I don't want to take those." She took them out of my hand and hurled them in the corner.

"My husband will be back… my husband," the wife bellowed in a hysterical frenzy.

"Deputy Sheriff Roman," I yelled, as she tried to grab Chica by the arm, tugging her violently away from me and yelling at her.

The officer raced through the door. "Back off," he motioned to the wife.

She froze, loosening her grip in defeat.

Without looking back I rushed Chica down the stairs and into the investigator's car. Every vehicle that pulled into the street made my heart skip a beat as I pictured an irate Jose Tecum leaping out and running towards us.

"Chica," I told her, "This nice woman is going to take you to a safe place. No one can hurt you or your family. I will see you soon," I reassured her. "I promise."

She hugged me tight. "Thank you!" she whispered. My legs threatened to give out as the adrenaline subsided and the car drove off, Chica waving at me from the passenger seat until they were out of sight.

Deputy Sheriff Roman stood next to me in the street. "Well done Anna…good job." I turned and hugged him. It wasn't a very professional thing to do, but at that moment, I didn't care. I was just so relieved to have gotten her out.

Back at the office, I didn't know whom to call. This situation was very different from any other that I had come across. I was told by the Sheriff officers, "This is out of our jurisdiction. You'll have to call Border Patrol." People told me, "You don't have to follow-up on that job." But I knew that I did have to follow up. My lieutenant said, "Just call Border Patrol, and we can send her back." But I remembered that Chica said that she was kidnapped. I wanted to do more than just send her back. I called Border Patrol for advice and to ask who could help me with this case.

I called the nearest Border Patrol office in Fort Lauderdale, advising them of the incident. I explained to them exactly what I had—a girl who had been kidnapped—and asked what I needed to do. The officer told me he would contact someone to follow up the investigation. Finally feeling more relaxed, I set about documenting my case notes. However, before leaving the office for the night, FBI Special Agent Ed Geiger called me. The phone was silent as he listened intently to what had gone on.

He was very nice and told me he needed to see Chica as soon as possible. The next couple of days were just as hectic as we did our best to ensure Chica was safe and out of harm's way. It wasn't easy.

Jose Tecum was used to getting his way and wasn't letting her go without a fight. He went to the office at the Shelter for Abused Women in Immokalee saying that his niece had been taken away by some woman at the Sheriff's Office and he was trying to see if they knew where she was so he could get her back. Luckily, Chica was at another safe place and not at the shelter. She was out of harm's way.

I settled back into my routine, aching back and all—oblivious to the magnitude of the situation. Everything got back to normal until I got another call from the FBI Special Agent Ed Geiger.

"Anna," he said. "We have Jose Tecum in custody. Do you realize you rescued a human trafficking victim?"

"What is that?" I innocently replied.

"A slavery victim!"

The flood of emotion returned. I slumped back in my chair, as though someone had punched me hard in the stomach. *I feel like a slave.* Chica's words rang in my head.

"And beat this," he added. "We found a lock of her hair in a plastic case in his wallet. He confessed he has a spell on her and her family."

I fell completely silent, too shocked to speak.

"Anna? Are you okay?"

"Yea, yea," I eventually muttered.

I found it hard to believe that all of Chica's story stacked up, every word proved to be true. He had kidnapped her, raped her, and dragged her halfway across the country. Even the part about how he convinced his own wife Chica was only there to pay off a debt to the family by working in the tomato field. The woman had no idea who Chica really was or that her husband was forcing Chica to have sex at night, until of course the night she caught them together.

When the news of the story broke in my office, my colleagues treated me like some kind of celebrity; me, a modern day emancipator. It was almost too much to take in.

Although I checked on Chica and thought of her constantly, after a while everything pretty much went back to normal, and I carried on with my life. My husband was getting more than irritated with me as I came up with every excuse in the book not to go and get my back looked at. The Advil I took religiously, hoping for even a little relief, had little effect. With Christmas only a few weeks away, I promised myself I would go see the doctor as soon as the holidays were over. In the meantime I did my best to hide the pain from my husband and carry on with work and family life.

I didn't make it to Christmas. One evening driving home, I had a sudden sharp stabbing pain through my lower back. I pulled over on the hard shoulder of the busy highway as cars whizzed past. I had my cell phone and radio with me, but I just wanted to get home and I didn't want to call dispatch and have them send EMS to help me. I continued home. It took forever, as I stopped every few miles until the pain subsided enough to continue. To be honest, I'm not even sure how I got there safely.

Doubled up, I almost crawled in through the front door. My husband gasped on seeing me.

"It's okay," I muttered, "I'm just going to lie down."

The next day I felt a little better and went to work. My husband had enough, thankfully, and decided to take action. He made me a doctor's appointment with an urologist. He drove me to the hospital himself, ignoring my protests.

After a series of tests, the doctor told me my left kidney had a severe infection.

"How long will it take to clear up?" my husband asked.

The doctor shook his head, "It's too late. We need to remove it as soon as possible to prevent the infection from spreading to the right kidney."

Two weeks before Christmas, I lay on the operating table ready to go into surgery. The operation was a full success.

"You're so lucky to be alive," my chastising, but thankful, husband kept reminding me when I came to.

I was released from hospital a week before Christmas, and I spent the next three months totally out of commission. My husband, as usual, was there for me. Physically, he spent as much time by my bedside as he could, while still making sure our three children, Gigi, Rob, and Lori were well taken care of. He was my Superman.

My colleagues were also wonderful, showering me with gifts and prayers. I lost track of Chica's case, but I thought about her every day.

Returning to work part-time in early March, I spent most of my first few weeks in the office near my home in Naples. It was a nice relaxing environment to work, so different from the manic workload of Immokalee, but I couldn't wait to get back there. After two days, I asked my sergeant to drive me to the Immokalee office to get all of my files and to see my co-workers. I wanted to thank them for being so kind to me. I had a surprise when I arrived. "Welcome Back" banners adorned the walls; a bouquet of flowers and lots of hugs and tears were waiting for me.

Then my attention turned to Chica. I got hold of Agent Geiger who soon brought me up to speed on the case. Everything seemed to be fine and progressing well. The FBI reached out to the Immokalee farm workers coalition which assisted them in getting Chica a home. In fact everything moved pretty fast, unbelievably fast. By the end of August, I found myself subpoenaed in court in Fort Myers as a witness for the case. The case was seen as influential in the Trafficking Victims Protection Act of 2000 (TVPA) that was passed by Congress shortly after Jose Tecum's arrest.

In a side room in the courthouse, Chica sat next to me. She looked so much better, so healthy and so beautiful, dressed in her native costume—hand selected and flown in from Guatemala for the occasion. I hadn't seen her since she was driven away on that fateful day. We hugged and held hands the entire time. Her parents were there too and they both hugged me, tearfully thanking me for rescuing their daughter.

Events in the courtroom over the three days proved stressful for everyone. While I sat outside waiting for my turn to give evidence, Chica took the stand.

Halfway through her testimony Tecum stood up and started yelling threats at her in their native language, K'iche.

"No I'm not lying," Chica mumbled, "I'm not." She looked around the court room.

Tecum yelled louder, pointing his finger at her, his face screwed up tightly. Judge John Steele stopped proceedings immediately and told the clerk of the court to take out the jury and Chica. Once they were outside, he turned to the defendant.

"Mr. Tecum," he almost stood up to attention. "You may speak to your attorney. You may not otherwise speak in court, and you may not address the witness. Do you understand?"

Tecum and his attorney both nodded their heads.

"Because if you continue," the judge added, "I will have you removed from this courtroom."

Outside Chica sat with me, sobbing into my arms.

"Don't worry," I assured her. "He's got no power over you anymore."

After he had given a stern warning to Tecum and his attorney, the judge called everyone back inside. Re-energized after our little chat, Chica handled the rest of her questioning with grace and strong character. Not only speaking confidently but also standing her ground very well when the defense lawyer did his best to convince the jury that Chica had come to the United States willingly with Jose Tecum.

When it came my turn to testify, I stood staring out at Jose Tecum. It was the first time I had seen him. I'm not sure why, but he didn't look as I expected him to look. He was small in size; thin and wiry too, his eyes black, scary looking, his hair thinning on the top of his head. His eyes bore into me full of hatred. I could understand why Chica and her family felt so intimidated. I did my best to ignore him, despite his stares, and stated all I knew about Chica and her terrible plight.

His defense attorney tried to discredit me with his very first question. "How could you have communicated so well with the girl in question since you do not speak K'iche, Mrs. Rodriguez?" he asked me.

Obviously he hadn't done his homework. "We spoke in Spanish," I replied, "I'm originally from Puerto Rico….Spanish is my native language." He seemed quite stunned with my response, and he sat down immediately.

After my testimony, I stayed in the courtroom, feeling rather drained but relived. I sat near the front and watched the proceedings. I couldn't get over just how much media attention there was in the room. There had been lots of hype around the case, lots of coverage in the newspapers and on the TV, not just in this area but throughout the country.

When Jose Tecum took the stand, eerie silence filled the room. When he began to speak, even his voice sounded evil, as if it would somehow burrow under my skin and nibble away at my flesh.

He began by denying he had taken Chica from her family without her or their consent. "She had come with me because she wanted to," he lied. "Her father wanted me to take her." He talked on and on, lie after lie pouring out of him.

The more he talked, the deeper he dug his own grave. No, more than just digging it, the longer he went on, he actually jumped in and started to fill the dirt back on top of himself.

"I would never hurt her," he admitted to the jury, "because I loved her like a daughter."

For some bizarre reason his attorney let him continue to talk and talk and talk. Finally he stunned everyone in the room. "I loved her and just wanted her to be my wife."

I could see his attorney put his head in his hands, defeat written over his face.

If his rant wasn't damaging enough, a video taken by the FBI of Chica's village in Guatemala, proved to be the final nail in Tecum's coffin. His lawyer had attempted to depict his client as an illiterate tomato picker who could never have plotted something so elaborate. However, the video clips revealed Tecum to be a wealthy man back in his village. It showed the massive estate he owned, surrounded by the poor shacks of the other villagers including Chica's parents' home.

Within a few hours of deliberation, the jury returned to announce their guilty verdict. Everyone cheered. Chica raced over to me and grabbed me in a tight embrace. Meanwhile the unrepentant Tecum loudly claimed his love for Chica as two officers escorted him out of the courtroom in handcuffs. He was prosecuted under the slavery laws of the United States, as well as several other counts including kidnapping, sale into involuntary servitude, bringing in and harboring aliens, fraud and misuse of visa and permits. Later his wife was charged and convicted of withholding information, but she was freed after six months.

When Judge Steele addressed Jose Tecum he told him: "If I had the power to change the guidelines, you would rot in hell!" Because of the sentencing guidelines for federal charges, Tecum received an eight-year sentence.

When Chica saw Tecum shackled, she had the biggest smile on her face. She turned to me, grabbing my hand and said, "He's going to pay every single day, for every tear and for every misery he put me through." Chica never talked about Jose Tecum again.

Lou de Baca, the Senior Special Counsel of the U.S. Department of Justice Civil Rights Division, came up to me and shook my hand and thanked me for having the sixth sense to realize something was wrong in the first place. "Anna, this case will make the U.S. history books."

And Lou de Baca was right. U.S. v. JOSE TECUM went a long way to help pass the T1 visa bill.

Human trafficking suddenly became the hot topic. Everyone seemed to be talking about it. David Brinkley interviewed me and wrote a piece about the case and human slavery for the *New York Times*. I also received a "command recognition" award by Sheriff Don Hunter for my involvement.

And the excitement didn't stop there. Several days later, I got a phone call from The Department of Justice, telling me the U.S. Attorney General John Ashcroft was going to sign the T1 visa protection act in Washington, which allowed victims who were rescued to stay in the United States for at least three years with the possibility of permanent residency. He wanted everyone involved in the Tecum case to be at the press conference on January 16, 2002.

I was honored and incredibly humbled. I felt so privileged. What I did wasn't anything that any other compassionate human being would not have done in the circumstances. I was just in the right place at the right time.

On the morning of my flight into Washington to witness the historical event, I didn't feel well. I convinced myself it was nerves or a twenty-four-hour virus. Yet again my caring husband wasn't taking any chances. On the way, he took me to see our doctor just in case. And after the kidney incident, I knew better than to argue with him.

After some poking and prodding, the doctor sat us both down. I squeezed my husband's hand tightly, nearly crushing it. I expected the worst, and I could tell by my husband's features he was also concerned.

"Mrs. Rodriguez, I'm afraid your stomach virus will disappear in about eight and-a-half months."

My husband and I looked at each other confused.

"Mrs. Rodriguez," the doctor added, "Congratulations! You're pregnant."

The color drained from my face in an instant. Shock replaced my fears. My oldest child was twenty-five years old! Then I fell apart, weeping uncontrollably; happiness and bittersweet thoughts of Gabriel, the baby boy I lost, overcame me. My husband wrapped his arms around me and wept openly.-

"I better not go to Washington," I said to him when we got ourselves back together and strolled out into the sunshine.

He stopped me. "You are," he insisted. "You deserve to go; now no arguing. None of this would be happening without you. Now go enjoy it."

I smiled at him, kissing him and giving him a hug. "I love you," I whispered.

Still in shock, he dropped me off at Fort Myers International Airport. There I met with FBI Special Agent Ed Geiger, who had become a dear friend. Chica was there also. I hadn't seen them both since the sentencing, although Chica and I frequently talked on the phone. She stood there smiling, her head held high. She was a million miles away from the downhearted young girl of not so many months ago. Now she was happily married to a lovely young man. What's more she had a six-month-old baby boy on her hip. She named him Eddie after the FBI agent.

I hugged her and the baby tight. 'Guess what?' I whispered in her ear.

"What?" she said pulling away surprised.

"I'm pregnant." I confessed sheepishly.

She put her hand to her mouth as tears rolled down her cheeks.

"Me too," she cried.

I started to cry. I knew this was God's way. He had blessed us both with children after our devastating losses.

"Oh boy, just what I need. Two hormonal sick women next to me on the plane," responded FBI Special Agent Ed Geiger.

"This will be good training for you," I joked.

Despite Chica's fear of flying, or of the big evil bird as she called it, and my frequent trips to the restroom to be sick, we made it to Washington safe and sound later that cold rainy night.

The hotel we stayed in was gorgeous. Located right in the center of the city, it had an impressive entrance hall with enormous chandeliers positioned overhead. People buzzed around us, coming and going in all directions. Chica's mouth dropped open as we sauntered in arm in arm. I don't think she had ever seen anything as grand in her young life. The joyful staff there treated us like royalty. The rooms they gave us were just as splendid. Chica cried when I explained that the room was just for her and no one else was going to use her bathroom.

After a nervous and sleepless night for me, we all headed to the Department of Justice Office where the ceremony was taking place. It was nerve racking. People milled everywhere, media and cameras crowded at the back of the plush room.

In my rush to get ready I hadn't noticed Chica was wearing jeans and a shirt. They were neat and tidy but I could see by the expression on the face of the federal prosecutor when she saw Chica walking in with me that it wasn't what she was expecting.

"Haven't you got anything else?" the prosecutor asked, shaking her head.

I translated. Chica shook her head. The ceremony was about to start, and it was too late to go and go buy something.

"Put this on," the prosecutor handed over her raincoat. "And don't take it off."

Confused, Chica did what she was told. I felt so sorry for her. It was two sizes too big, and she could have wrapped it around her twice over. It made her looked so tiny, so helpless, standing there amongst some of the most powerful people in the country. I was nervous. I could only begin to imagine how Chica was feeling.

It was time for the press conference and they had us walk in and stand behind the Attorney General. Chica was seated in the back of the room and no one noticed that she was the person the Attorney General was talking about.

Attorney General Ashcroft thanked everyone by name for helping free the victim involved in the Tecum case. I shook in my shoes. Although standing with all the bright lights was making me feel dizzy, and I thought I was going to faint, it was an incredible experience.

"The Tecum arrest," Attorney General Ashcroft added, "was a major breakthrough in the war against human trafficking, and it was because of cases like this that I can stand before you in this packed room and sign the T1 visa protection act."

The audience erupted in applause. I looked over at Chica, looking so small and innocent dressed in the oversized raincoat, amongst the press who didn't know who she was. I smiled. The sad part was the media lost track of the importance of the statements made by the Attorney General because that same day the Unabomber was arrested.

When the Attorney General finished, we were all led to a side room where he handed the pen he used to sign the bill to Chica and said softly. "Chica, with this pen I have signed your freedom. Welcome to the United States. But remember you must guard this pen with your life," he joked, wrapping it in a handkerchief and handing it to her.

I wept as a smiling Chica accepted the pen.

Even today she keeps the pen in the original handkerchief and guards it with her life.

Treated Like a Dog

After unknowingly rescuing Chica, I began to look at life through a different set of eyes. My outlook on the world changed. I started to question everything, to look at people differently. Was the teenager sulking in the grocery store just a moody youth embarrassed to be seen in public with her father or was there something darker under the surface? Were the workers tolling away in the fruit fields there to earn money for their family or forced to do it to pay off a debt?

I, probably like most, always assumed slavery was a word used in a much different era, a word and a mind-set that had been abolished a long time ago. Human trafficking didn't go on in America. It was one of those atrocities suffered far away, in less westernized, less educated and godless countries

But I was so wrong; I had discovered a modern-day slave in my own Florida back yard. The experience spurred me on to find out more about the subject of human trafficking and slavery. I investigated as much as I could. It became an obsession and what I uncovered shocked and disgusted me.

Human trafficking is just another word for modern-day slavery, a twenty-first century global concern that has no geographic, age, race or gender boundaries. Victims of human trafficking are vulnerable and come from impoverished countries. Surprisingly, it isn't all about the sex trade. It's a lot more widespread and diverse. Forced labor, also known as bonded labor or debt labor, is one of the biggest forms of modern day slavery. Victims, like Chica, are fooled into believing they owe their abductor money that they need to pay back before they can be freed. Of course, the plan is for the victim never to pay off their arrears as the trafficker continues to add fees for this, costs for that. They are forever in their abductor's debt.

The scale of the problem is unbelievable. Human trafficking is one of the biggest and most profitable illegal industries in the world today. It is estimated between 600,000 and two million people are trafficked annually on a worldwide basis. That means between twenty-one and twenty-seven million people are locked into slavery throughout the world. Where are all these invisible people? Where do they come from? How does something on this big a scale go undetected, or is it just ignored, forgotten, or brushed under the political carpet.

In the United States alone it is estimated that around two and a half million victims are trafficked into slavery. Florida, with the combination of agriculture, tourism, construction and service industries, has a massive supply of migrant workers making it one of the top five states in the country for human trafficking.

It began to make sense when I started to comprehend how much money was involved in this evil trade. It is estimated to be joint second in the most lucrative illegal business for organized crime selling firearms. These two are still behind the infamous drug trade, but human trafficking is quickly closing the gap. Profit figures as high as thirty-four billion dollars are reported. Most legitimate companies can't boast such earnings.

Human trafficking's increasing popularity comes from the fact that, unlike drug and arms dealers, traffickers can continue to exploit their merchandise year in and year out. Once a line of cocaine is snorted, it is gone. When a gun is sold, it's sold. However a human being can be used, abused, and sold many times over. And the supply is plentiful to satisfy the ever-growing demand. There's a conveyor belt of victims pouring into the country. It rolls on and on without stopping. Some of them are forced to come here; others promised a life that they can only dream of living in America.

The numbers are staggering. For example, when I first began researching human trafficking 1,700 children were reported missing each day in America alone. Today it's closer to 2,300 children per day. Also, a mere forty-eight hours after they go missing, at least two-thirds of them are abducted and recruited into the sex or labor trade industry.

Children are easy pickings for the human vultures who prey on them. Five years ago, the average age of entry into prostitution was fifteen, which is a shocking enough statistic. Today it has dropped dramatically; the average age is twelve for girls and eleven for boys.

Another thing I soon discovered about the dark and dangerous world of human trafficking is that although many of the victims are poor, uneducated or from deprived backgrounds, in most cases it has very little to do with class, creed or color. The individuals, however, that profit from this despicable trade, in one way or another, are not poor.

There is such a wide range of individuals and businesses involved in the trade it's unimaginable. The scale of operations is vast and extremely diverse. There are large international organized criminal syndicates with well-stocked portfolios of illegal activities such as human, drug and gun trafficking, grand scale operations making maximum profits out of misery and death. Sophisticated and modern equipment is used; intelligent people run the operation like a CEO would run any business, or in many cases like a general would organize an army. They use staffing agents that, knowingly or unknowingly, provide cheap labor for various types of work from agricultural or construction, to the restaurant industry or janitorial businesses. These operations prove a perfect breeding ground for slavery with low paid manual jobs and with little chance of getting investigated. On the other end of the scale there are much smaller but just as ruthless "mom and pop" family operations.

And surprisingly, it's not just men responsible for running the human trafficking industry. Nowadays more and more women are being drawn in, often in the role of madams in the countless brothels springing up around the country or as recruiters exploiting other women to cross the borders.

And I quickly found, slavery is not only about immigrants working in the fields or girls forced to sell their bodies. It is also about those enslaved inside places we wouldn't think or maybe places we just don't want to believe. It's often these cases that rarely anything is written about. They are a mass of invisible victims working as domestic servants in luxurious homes or mansions throughout the country. Most times, the traffickers are of the same nationality but with a social position or education superior to their victims.

Consequently the next case I stumbled across fell into the "I would never have suspected that to happen in a place like this" category.

Again, like Chica's case, I got a call from a concerned road patrol officer who had been called to a disturbance involving a wealthy couple and some members of a local church. After the police officer arrived at the incident and began to interview the people involved, he quickly concluded there was a lot more brewing below the surface than he first expected. Something wasn't right. Because of my newfound fame as the "human trafficking expert", I was the one who received his call.

Being new and very much green behind the ears, I immediately thought of another Chica; a poor girl living in a small apartment in the middle of a small town.

I was wrong. This time, I found myself working a case at a large mansion on the so-called right side of town. I realized as I stood amongst the wealthy community, this was a bigger problem than I ever could have imagined.

Alicia, a forty-seven-year old woman, was desperate to find a good job in the United States to help pay for the repairs to her family's home in El Salvador after it had been badly damaged during an earthquake. With large parts of her village destroyed, she was more than pleased when she had a telephone conversation with a man from southwest Florida concerning a job as a live-in maid for his family. Although hesitant to leave her family, especially at such a terrible time, the promise of a two-year contract with a regular four hundred dollar a week paycheck, plus room and board and medical coverage was just too much of an attraction to turn down. It wasn't what her family wanted—they didn't want her to leave at all—but it was what they needed at the time.

Alicia, a devout Christian, was painfully shy, very smart and selfless. She had a business administration degree and was extremely hard working. She was the type of person always willing to put others before herself.

Never before venturing out of her country, she naively turned up at the Miami airport in the United States holding a sign with the name of her new employer written on it. Pedro Moran was there to meet and greet her. He was holding a sign with her name on it. The grey-haired man was well dressed in a light coloured suit and expensive leather shoes, obviously wealthy, full of confidence and extremely pleasant.

Alicia was secretly relieved. She knew she could never be too careful when travelling to a new country, especially as a woman. Moran drove her to Naples where he lived.

Things got even better when they pulled up to the house where she would be working. It was beautiful, a $2.5 million dollar mansion. She smiled as they drove through the large electric gates, into a world she'd never imagined in her wildest dreams. A world of heated swimming pools and large well-kept gardens was a million miles away from the conditions she was used to and a lifetime away from the poverty of her village.

Moran's wife, Ali, rushed out to meet her. She too was immaculately clothed in a flowing bright coloured dress and had gold rings on her fingers. She seemed very pleasant and although she didn't speak any Spanish, she made a big fuss. Ali showed Alicia around the immaculately decorated house, including her room. A while later the wife took her to the supermarket and told her to pick out anything she liked.

That night, they had a meal together like one big happy family.

The very next day, Alicia began her work. Her duties were varied; they included cleaning the house and the garage, washing clothes, ironing, some cooking and taking care of the couple's two children and the dogs. There was a lot to do, but she didn't mind the hard work. The only thing she didn't really like were the two intimidating dogs, Doberman Pinschers, that the family owned that would growl at her as she hurried past them.

However, she didn't complain. She knew it could have been a lot worse and more importantly, she knew every penny she earned was going to be sent back to her own family. The agreed fee of four hundred a week was more than she would ever earn back in her homeland, plus she had been promised an increase of fifty dollars a month after six months and all her medical bills would be covered if required. She was also told that she would receive another fifty dollars after one year.

She worked hard, trying her best to impress her new employers. Everything seemed to be going well. But after a week, the situation changed.

"Don't clean it like that," the wife got angry as Alicia swept the kitchen floor. "Do it right."

Alicia started sweeping faster, not really understanding what she was doing wrong.

"No, I said," the wife starting screaming and yelling uncontrollably. "Do it properly." She stormed out upset, leaving Alicia wondering why she had upset her for no apparent reason.

That same night, Ali ignored Alicia and did not speak to her at all. The next morning, she started yelling and flailing her arms at Alicia again. Sometimes she even threw things— like plates, shoes and once a glass ashtray— at Alicia. Alicia would always apologize profusely and profess, in her best broken English, to try even harder, but the harder she tried, the worse it got.

One morning Ali marched into Alicia's comfortable bedroom. "Okay… you are moving… get your stuff."

Still half asleep, Alicia asked her where to.

"Just shut up and follow me."

She took her down to a tiny room next to the swimming pool. "In here… this is where you will sleep for now on."

"Why?"

"Cause I said… now put your things away and get to work."

There was no air conditioning in the small pool shed where the rafts and pool supplies were stored. She had just a rollaway bed that could be folded up and moved. The bed had a very thin mattress, which she believed contributed to her back problems. The room smelled of chemicals from the swimming pool that caused her to feel ill. She had little to no privacy at all.

"The dogs lived in better conditions," she later told me.

Ali's attitude towards her got worse. She would often leave the door to Alicia's new bedroom open. The mosquitoes and other bugs that flew into the room all day bit her as she slept. Her arms soon became covered in sores. Ali didn't like the look of the bites, and she told Alicia to cover herself. So she was forced to wear long sleeves and pants even in the extreme heat.

Every time the couple had dinner parties, which was about once a month, Alicia had to move her stuff out of her new room until the party was over so the guests would not realize where Alicia was forced to sleep. Then she was ordered to clean up the mess in the house and move her things back into the room. She had to stay up until everything was cleaned up. Some nights she didn't get to bed until the early hours and was still expected to do her usual duties the next morning. Her normal working hours were long, from seven in the morning until seven at night. So depending on Ali's mood or when the parties ended Alicia sometimes worked until one in the morning.

Before she took the job and had come to the United States, she spoke to Pedro Moran on the phone. She had told him that she was very devoted to religion. He had agreed that Alicia could have Sundays off, from noon until six in the evening, to attend church service. But that changed too. Her day off soon got limited to three hours, noon to three o'clock and even with that, there was a catch.

Ali told her that she wanted all of the church members full names and addresses and other documentation like telephone numbers, driver's license and social security numbers before she would allow her to attend. Reluctantly, and rather surprisingly, the members agreed but only after the pastor persuaded them to comply. The Morans told her that they were responsible for her before the United States Government and that is why they needed this information. The wife also warned Alicia not to get friendly with anyone at the church or there would be repercussions.

Each day around the house her tasks became harder and the list of things to do grew bigger and bigger. On top of all that work, she was instructed to clean a neighbour's house as well for no extra pay.

It was hard work, but when she complained, Alicia was shown a photograph of a police officer the couple said was their son, a local sheriff. "If you don't do as we say… he'll make you disappear," the wife glared at her.

"What do you mean?" Alicia naively asked.

"You'll find out," Ali snickered.

Other times they threatened to call the Immigration and Naturalization Service (INS) and have her put in jail if she did anything wrong or complained at all.

Although they never physically hit her, they threatened her daily with violence. Moran often boasted how he had once used a baseball bat on someone that he didn't like and had gotten away with it because his son, the police officer, had so much power in the area. Moran implied he would do the same to her if she crossed him. He often got drunk and made advances on her when his wife wasn't around. Alicia declined. But it didn't stop him from touching and groping her at every opportunity.

The way they treated her worsened with each passing day. The guarantee of a pay raise after six months and the medical coverage that had been promised never materialised. She began to develop pains in her arms, shoulders and lower back, and she told Pedro that she was not feeling well. There was no offer to help with the medical expenses. She couldn't afford the cost of medical care so she suffered in pain. One day she became ill and couldn't get out of bed. The couple finally agreed to call the doctor. A week later, after she was feeling better, Alicia was told the doctor bill would be debited from her month's wages.

Everyday Ali would take her moods out on Alicia. She screamed for no apparent reason, spitting her anger at her when things weren't done immediately or how she wanted them. On several occasions, neighbours and workers heard the commotion, but nothing was done and nothing was reported.

Ali began following her around the house, checking her work. She called her lazy and made her work faster. On Ali's command, the two dogs would race at Alicia and pin her up to the wall, teeth snarling, drool dripping from their mouths. These Dobermans were trained attack dogs. They often bit her legs. She was scared stiff, fearing she would get ripped apart. But the dogs were totally different when the Morans were not around. Alicia was able to bath and feed them without any problem.

Soon, cameras were installed everywhere and doors and gates were wired to the alarm system. Ali monitored Alicia's every movement from her office. She didn't have a minute for herself. Whenever she finished one job, Ali would show up to instruct her to do another.

Long gone were the trips to the grocery store where she picked out what she liked to eat. In fact she wasn't even allowed to have breakfast or lunch anymore and most of the time she was only given scraps from the dinner table or half-eaten sandwiches for dinner. Desperate and hungry, she started hiding leftover food in a cupboard, but Ali found it and fed it to the dogs in front of Alicia.

"Don't ever do that again," she warned her, "Or I will give my son a call."

She lost a considerable amount of weight, her face thin and drawn as if she was suffering from a major illness. She was skin and bone. Someone at the church, who hadn't been there in a while, didn't recognise Alicia when he saw her. When he realized, he assumed Alicia must have been sick.

The use of a phone was denied and later all phones in the house were disconnected except for the one in the Moran's office. When she wanted to call her son or her daughter in El Salvador, she would make these calls on Sunday with a phone card she purchased through the assistance of church members.

Prior to leaving for the United States, Alicia's mother was very sick. She had gotten even worse and Alicia's sister managed to contact Alicia to tell her. Alicia begged the couple to let her go back home. Although she didn't have the money, surprisingly, the couple finally agreed she could go back but only with the stipulation that Pedro Moran accompany her. Alicia didn't really have a choice. They had told Alicia that housekeepers in the past had left after only a month or two of working for them.

The couple paid for the trip that took them from Miami to Guatemala City then to San Salvador, in June of 2000. Moran was never far from Alicia's side, always whispering to her that something bad would happen to her or her family if she told anyone about what was going on. Despite all she'd been through, on their return, she thanked the couple for being so understanding and generous. Sadly her mother died not long after she returned to Florida, in July of 2000. During her time of grief, she was told by Ali she now owed $1,470.00 for her trip. Without any discussion, her wages were reduced further. She was now down to two hundred dollars a month to help pay off her debt.

Extremely upset, she still didn't tell the members of the church, her only contact with the outside world, what was going on. Ali had warned her that if they caused any trouble, they would face the wrath of Pedro Moran and since some of them were illegal aliens, she didn't want to get them in trouble. But because of Alicia's now shocking appearance, the members were highly suspicious that things just weren't right. They fed her food when she attended service and questioned her endlessly looking for answers for what they could do to help.

Alicia often shrugged, too scared to talk to them just in case.

Every week her debts grew bigger and the verbal abuse she had to endure became worse. Alicia was at a breaking point. She started keeping her own monthly records of what she was owed and what they had deducted from her unfairly. One morning Ali Moran found the book and burned it.

Another Sunday some of the church members confronted Ali as she arrived to pick Alicia up. Ali went crazy, shouting and yelling outside the church doors that her son was a police officer and would make them all pay. She told them she would start a scandal and get them all deported, that there would be personal hell to pay for each and every one of them and that the church itself would be destroyed.

Despite the threats and fear of repercussion, her church family, with the support of the pastor, concocted a plan to help Alicia. They believed it was their Christian duty.

The next Sunday, the Morans dropped Alicia off at church and waited in their car. As soon as Alicia went in through the front door, she was escorted out through the back door and to a safe place at one of the family's homes.

When the service ended and Alicia didn't appear, the couple became irate.

"Where is she?" Moran shouted and screamed at the church members. "Tell me now or I will have you all deported."

Some of the church members ran away, scared. The Morans went to every address on the list they had been provided previously, banging on doors and screaming for Alicia to come out. Eventually they tracked her down at an elderly couple's apartment about a mile away from the church.

"Let us in," Moran yelled as they both banged on the door.

Ali screamed wildly, threatening to call the police and get everyone inside arrested and deported.

A neighbor heard all the commotion and called the police. Two officers arrived on the scene, and, after a quick investigation, one of the officers called me.

At the time the couple wasn't charged and hurriedly left to go home. The next day the couple disappeared. They told a neighbor they were going on a vacation for a few weeks but didn't say where.

I was called by the responding officers to the family's apartment complex off Pine Ridge Road in Naples next to an old YMCA. I went up stairs to the apartment were Alicia was sitting at the table quietly crying and visibly shaking.

"Hello... I'm Anna," I tried to comfort her, "I'm here to help you."

She didn't smile at all and I could see the fear and suspicion in her eyes. She was so thin I could see her bones.

"I wasn't always this thin." She must have seen me staring. "They... they... never gave me any food... maybe once or twice a week, maybe a hot dog or a hamburger... I've lost too much weight... I feel so tired."

She lifted her sleeve up.

"Oh my God," I blurted the words out without thinking. "What's happened to your arms?" The skin on her arms was a terrible mess, plastered with scars.

"The insects and bugs come into my room and did this." She pulled up her T-shirt. Horrifically the rest of her body wasn't much better with bites covering nearly every inch of skin. She explained about the room by the swimming pool and how the insects ate her alive each night.

Sitting in the kitchen, shivering, wrapped in a blanket, she told me the entire story. "I'm not going back to them. You can't make me," she kept repeating to me.

"You don't have to go back to them. You will never go back to them," I assured her.

"Good... because I don't want to die. If I go back I will."

"Alicia... we will look after you. No one's going to harm you again." I talked to her, and even held her in my arms as she sobbed.

I watched her eat a plate of food and not talk or look up until it was all gone. I tried to stay with her at the apartment as late as I possibly could. At night, Alicia told me, she found it difficult to sleep, and when she did, her sleep was riddled with nightmares. She constantly woke screaming, yelling, covered in sweat, even after it was discovered that the Moran's son wasn't really a police officer.

I called the FBI and on the same day, and Special Agent Ed Geiger responded immediately. I acted as a translator as Alicia told her whole story to Agent Geiger.

I never actually met the Morans at all. About a month after Alicia was found and identified as a trafficking victim, the FBI discovered the couple had not only returned but had brought with them another victim from El Salvador. The FBI special agent called me again and asked me to accompany him to the house. When we arrived at the residence, I noticed the security cameras glaring down at me. The FBI was told by neighbors that the suspects were out of the country and the housekeeper was home alone.

We went to the gate's intercom and I did the talking since I spoke Spanish. The lady answered and, when I asked her for the woman of the house, she said that no one was home. I lied and told her I had a packet for her and I needed to drop it off. There was silence for a few minutes but then she appeared from the front door and walked towards the gate. She was short with brown curly hair, around fifty years old, and wearing an apron. She opened the gate and I asked her if we could talk to her.

She agreed. She told me that she was visiting her long lost uncle. Knowing full well she was lying, I asked her how she found him. I continued translating for the FBI. Finally she told me she was hired as a nanny and that they told her to lie. She had no work authorization and came with her tourist visa. The FBI then told her about the fate of the last employee and she was shocked but still refused to go with us. She kept saying that they had cameras and she would be in trouble if they saw her talking with us. Finally I gave her my contact number and told her to call me if she needed help.

She never did. Two weeks later, she was beaten quite badly by Mrs. Moran but managed to escape to a neighbor's house. Thankfully, the neighbor took pity on her and bought her a bus ticket to New York so she could stay with her niece. Her niece, shocked at her appearance and the stories she was told, made contact with us immediately. The FBI agent flew to New York to meet with her.

With this extra evidence, I thought the conviction of the couple would be no problem. Unfortunately, I was wrong. Unbelievably, the Morans were never even arrested, let alone charged with a crime. They disappeared again soon after. Some of the neighbors said they had left for Costa Rica. The reaction of the Department of Justice was a disappointment to me. The prosecutor stated that it was one word against another and that the couple had no criminal record. Even the FBI special agent was frustrated. He had done an outstanding investigation. To me it was an open and shut case, but the whole case was dismissed. Fortunately, however, the Department of Justice still certified the new maid as a victim of human trafficking, and she became eligible for a trafficking visa.

The compassion of the FBI special agent assigned to the case was amazing. He was transferred to DC, but the week before he left, we met with Alicia for lunch. When he was leaving, he handed her an envelope. "This is for you," he said and kissed her cheek. "Merry Christmas."

When I took Alicia home, she opened the card and found a hundred dollar bill. She started crying and kept saying that he made her feel like a normal person again.

I found a legal aid attorney for Alicia so she could get her T1 visa. It was an immigration agency that advocated for immigrants to help them obtain their immigration paperwork for the visa. The work was pro-bono, without charge to the client, and at that time that it was the only agency that was assisting human trafficking victims in the application for a T1 visa.   The process was taking much longer than it should have. Alicia and I kept calling, to be told over and over that they lost her paperwork!

After two and a half years of persistence on our part, the agency submitted the application. Then a couple of months later, Alicia called me. "I received a letter from US Citizenship and Immigration Services, and I don't know what it says because it's in English," she said. So I stopped by her apartment. When I read the letter, it was a denial because the agency had filed for the wrong application! They requested a Temporary Protection Status, which is offered for people from El Salvador. Even though I was not an attorney, I knew that Alicia did not qualify for that because she didn't meet the criteria for that type of visa.

So I called the agency, again reiterating that Alicia needed the T1 visa. The attorney told me that I needed to get a hold of the FBI agent because she had misplaced the paperwork (again!) I decided to try a different route.

I connected Alicia with a private immigration attorney instead. He was willing to assist Alicia with her immigration application pro-bono. Alicia set up the appointment with him, but when he called the former attorney, she was short and arrogant with him and said she needed to talk to Alicia. The former attorney left messages at Alica's home all day while Alicia was at work, reaching her after ten o'clock at night. She threatened Alicia with a call to immigration to have her deported if she worked with a different attorney.

I think that she was angry because Alicia outsmarted her and decided not to keep playing her game. These legal agencies receive state and federal funding to assist immigrants so they are compensated according to the number of people they help. She was more concerned about losing money. Alicia was just a number to her.

It is sad that these survivors are being re-victimized by the agencies that **claim** to assist victims of human trafficking.

Alicia's emotional scars took time to heal from all the psychological pain she endured. But slowly she started to get her life back on track. She was able to secure a work permit, and I helped her get a job. Later she found a small apartment and I couldn't resist taking her on a spending spree to get her furniture.

Two years after her rescue, Alicia met a widower from El Salvador and they fell in love. I remember meeting him at the office when he asked me for Alicia's hand in marriage. In tears he told me that his wife-to-be, Alicia, felt I was like a sister to her. We all hugged each other.

In October 2004, as a notary public in the State Of Florida, I performed the marriage ceremony between Alicia and Jose. As I stood there in front of them both, I couldn't help notice the transformation Alicia had undergone. She was no longer the shy, fearful shell I'd met in that apartment. She'd gained weight, and she looked so happy. It was a very emotional moment; we were both crying. It was one of the best moments of my life.

Alicia and I became very close and remain so today. She still says that I am her sister and guardian angel.

Alicia and Jose still live in Florida, still very much in love. They are legal residents of the United States and have their own business. Alicia is finally living the American dream.

The Mobile Brothel

In some quarters of today's society, the word pimp has suddenly become acceptable, even thought of as cool. TV programs such as *Pimp My Ride* glamorize it all, brainwashing teenagers into believing it's a word connected with something cool and hip. And it doesn't stop with TV shows. There are songs by world famous rappers that shamelessly glorify the pimp culture in their songs. Others, the same men who rightfully decry what happened in America before the abolition of slavery, boast of actually being pimps themselves before they became respectable and moved into large LA mansions. There are books written by street pimps telling about how to become one of them, as if it's a respectable career. One day I half-expect to see a copy of *The Dummies Guide to Becoming a Pimp* on the shelf at my local bookstore.

But it's not cool or hip at all. In fact, it's the total opposite. Pimping is all about destroying individuals in the name of making money. It's an evil trade where vile animals prey on their victims, exploiting other humans for their own gain.

These pimps pluck young girls and boys off the street or purchase them off poor families that are forced into selling their children to survive. They are easy prey. These creatures profit from individuals' misery, by selling something which shouldn't be for sale, by selling the innocence of young children, by ruining people's lives forever. I didn't realize until I started researching the subject that seventy percent of the victims are females and, incredibly, fifty-six percent of those victims are children under the age of consent.

Up to this point, my experience with human trafficking was limited to forced labor. And then I came face to face with dark world of the sex trade.

The sex trade contributes a devastating statistic to the underworld of human trafficking, with its exploitation totaling thirteen billion dollars annually, according to the International Labor Organization. Sadly with this trade, like most illegal operations, there are no boundaries to contain it, no rules, and no taboo areas. Adults and teenagers are lured or dragged in this world, as are, shockingly, even young children.

With the demand for sex growing, it's a simple case of economics. The pimps, like snake oil salesmen, are always looking for ways to exploit the market. The worrying fact is that there is a growing trend for younger merchandise in response to the buyer's demands for youth and purity.

Pimps are very focused individuals, knowing exactly what they want out of life and how to get it. Usually they're masters at manipulating. They create a web of lies and promises which lure the victims into their grip. Their plan is quite simple. They purposely go after victims with low self-esteem and try to quickly become like father figures to them, offering protection and much-needed love.

Often the security of becoming part of a larger "family" lures the victims into the pimp's web. Once caught, the victim is trapped, and it's almost impossible to get out. Fairy tales, like what Julia Roberts found herself in on the movie *Pretty Woman,* where she is whisked from the streets into the arms of a rich and famous Richard Gere, don't happen.

The pimps are ruthless creatures with a bag full of methods and techniques to win over their victims and rip out their souls. One of their techniques is to identify the physical and psychological needs of their victim. Once detected they quickly seek to fill the need of the person to win over their trust. If a child longs for the loving arms of a lost parent, they become the father figure. If it's a place to sleep the child needs, they provide a home, a shelter from the cold. The pimp's objective is simple— make the victim dependent on them.

With purpose and premeditation, they target vulnerable kids like runaways or cast-offs. Virgins are a particularly hot commodity as pimps are always on the lookout to maximize their profit potential. Recruiting locations also include areas like junior high and high schools, courtrooms and hallways of court buildings where teenagers find themselves alone and looking for someone to befriend. Or similar places like foster homes or group homes, bus stations, homeless shelters, and halfway houses. And there are always restaurants and bars, parks and playgrounds and shopping malls. The unfortunate opportunities are endless.

Most victims are groomed by their pimps in a sophisticated process. Grooming is largely a two-stage process prior to the girl being 'turned-out' on to the streets. First, the victim is made to feel attractive and wanted, to feel like a real person, someone of value. The pimps lavish them with money and gifts.

It is one of the pimp's greatest techniques, providing a sense of false love to the victim. They use this power and so-called wealth to "court" a girl. Rife with promises of a better life, fast money and a life of luxuries, the pimp is always careful to protect his real identity.

Once they've gone through stage one of the grooming process and the victim starts to believe her life isn't all that bad, the pimp will attempt to break the girl's will through physical, sexual and verbal abuse to prepare her for going out on the "game." The pimp will freely introduce a cycle of intimacy and violence, often regularly beating his "girl" up in public or putting her through bouts of torture like burning her skin with cigarettes or hot metal. They even stoop as low as setting up gang rapes where, after the event, the terrified victim relies on the pimp for protection. They use other techniques as well like starvation or drug addiction.

When they are in control of their victim, they use multiple means to maintain the domination like violence, debt bondage, threats against family and friends and intimidation. A pimp will make the victim refer to him exclusively as "daddy." She may not ever make eye contact with another pimp. There are even rules about where and how to stand on the sidewalk and the street, as indicated by the phrase "pimps up, hoes down". Women and girls must always exist in lower ways than the pimp, including standing on the street rather than the sidewalk. A woman or girl who ventures onto the sidewalk is severely reprimanded or forced into what is known as a pimp circle, which is where multiple pimps swarm the offender and hiss insults at her for the purposes of humiliation and intimidation.

When ready to earn money, victims are given quotas to achieve each and every night, which may go up in busy times but rarely come down when quiet. The pimps collect all the money, normally nothing is given back to the victims. If quotas are not met, the punishment includes beatings, rape, or being left out in the cold.

Like crafty businessmen, pimps often share tactics, assist each other and craft new techniques together for speeding up the process of grooming and getting more out of their resources. During this whole time of forced employment, they make sure to destroy their victims physically, psychologically and emotionally.

Iceberg Slim, a well-known pimp, said, "Fast, I got to find out the secrets of pimping. I really want to control the whole whore. I want to be the boss of her life, even her thoughts. I got to con them that Lincoln never freed the slaves."

Another pimp went on record to say, "You'll start to dress her, think for her, and own her. If you and your victim are sexually active, slow it down. After sex, take her shopping for one item. Hair and nails are fine. She'll develop a feeling of accomplishment. Then shopping after a month will be replaced with cash. The lovemaking turns into raw sex. She'll start to crave the intimacy and be willing to be back in your good graces. After you have broken her spirit, she has no sense of self-value. Now pimp, put a price tag on the item you have manufactured."

The sex trade is a seedy, disturbing world. The demand created by the customers or johns (as they are called by people working in the trade) help support the pimp's lifestyle. Web sites have sprung up on the Internet where johns and sex predators communicate. These sites detail locations of prostitution, massage parlors, brothels and sex tours.

In the Blackjack case in December of 2002, I discovered in graphic detail this deplorable form of trafficking. Conchita, a pretty eighteen-year-old girl met two men in her native Puebla, Mexico, while scrubbing floors and taking care of children. One of the men, Javier, with the help of his sisters, approached Conchita and promised her that she could earn lots of money working in a fancy restaurant in southwest Florida. She didn't want to go at first, but the promise of waiting tables for rich tourists and the thought earning big tips seemed like a good career move for a girl who was getting paid far less than ten thousand dollars per year.

A few weeks later, she was smuggled across the border to Fort Myers with some other women who had also been sold the same promises.

During the journey, Conchita soon became friendly with a nineteen-year-old named Theresa from a village about seventy miles from her own. The men treated them well, bought them food, told them stories of how other girls, whom they had gotten jobs, were now managers of their own restaurants or married with families in America. Conchita and Theresa talked excitedly about their new jobs and how they would meet up on a regular basis once they settled down. They soon became best friends.

When they arrived however, both Conchita and Theresa were in for a shock. There was no job waiting tables or serving coffee or even washing dishes. Almost immediately, the occupation they had been promised switched from waitress to full-time and full-on prostitute. They had been smuggled across the border by the *pollero,* or coyote, so they now had a smuggling debt. Their smuggling debt was about $2,500.

Overnight they found themselves entangled in a hardcore sex web that they couldn't get out of. Their traffickers, turned pimps, told Conchita she had to work for well over two years before she would be allowed to go back home with threats of harm or murder to her family if she ran away or told anyone.

She was forced to have sex with at least fifteen men a night, six days a week. On "special" occasions, like big football games or when business conferences came rolling into town, that number would climb to as high as thirty clients per night. The price for their service was twenty-one dollars (twenty for sex; a dollar for the condom) for ten to fifteen minutes, which of course went directly to the pimp with promise of food and clothes or for money to be wired to their families in Mexico.

The pimps made a fortune. The estimated revenues from trafficking per girl was about $375 to $500 per night, up to $182,500 per year per girl—and these two pimps had fifteen, sometimes twenty, in their stables at any one time, each seeing up to fifteen johns.-

Any complaints about the girl's performance resulted in brutal beatings. Conchita was beaten badly after a john complained to the pimp that she was cold during sex. She was thrown down the stairs, kicked and bitten on the leg. The next night she was quickly patched up and forced to go through her nightly duties or risk a beating with a "pimp stick", a coat hanger that has been unraveled and doubled over and used to beat the victim on the thighs leaving them with black and blue whip marks.

During the day, Conchita was kept locked away in a disgusting apartment near downtown Fort Myers. The walls and floors were filthy, clothes, cigarette butts and empty condom wrappers littered the worn and stained carpet. She slept in a fold-up bed or a bunk bed with six other girls in one small room. There was one toilet which often got blocked and the air conditioner never worked.

Phone calls were only allowed when one of the men was present. Knives were held up against her throat as she talked to loved ones back home to ensure she didn't say anything that would raise any suspicions. If she did say anything that was perceived as wrong, the call was promptly ended and she was immediately beaten on the spot.

She wasn't allowed to leave the house without the men.

At night she was moved into a beat-up white van, a mobile brothel.

The mobile brothel Conchita and Theresa were involved in travelled up to eighty miles a night to old warehouses, abandoned houses, or behind abandoned factories where the girls would have sex with johns in the back of the van, which was lined with stinking mattresses, in doorways or behind parked cars. Once the johns paid for the services, they were given a playing card as a token, which proved that he paid his fee. The john would hand the girl the card before the sex act.

Demand was plentiful, with their unique way of advertising the stolen goods. *Carne fresca*, meaning fresh meat, was written on small pieces of notebook paper with a phone number and posted in ethnic stores all over town to advertise the girls' services. Men would call to find out where the van would be heading that night. Apparently there was always a stream of men waiting as the mobile brothel pulled up.

After the sessions, the girls were taken back home for a little rest until it all started over again the next day. Conchita got to the point where she wanted to kill herself.

Then one night she finally had a stroke of luck. Six girls were moved in the white van to one of their regular destinations by two male guards. A few men were already waiting for them in an isolated parking lot. The traffickers had promoted the girls through the migrant community in Collier County but it still proved to be quite a slow night compared with other nights. The greedy pimp, Javier Rojas, decided to knock on the doors of a Sunshine Boulevard apartment block in Golden Gate to drum up some extra trade. In one apartment a twenty-year-old man was approached to see if he and his roommates wanted to have sex with some girls. After some discussion and bartering about price, they agreed.

When Javier brought the girls back, the twenty-year-old recognized Conchita as one of his old classmates from Puebla. Without making it too obvious, he quickly paid the pimp the twenty-one dollars and took her into his bedroom. He locked the door behind him and turned up the radio so her pimp waiting outside couldn't hear their conversation.

"Conchita, it's Pablo," he whispered.

She didn't recognize him at first.

"I was in school with you." He could tell by her appearance and lack of emotion that something wasn't right.

Suddenly as if a light came on, she hugged him. "Pablo! Help me… please… help me."

He checked the door again before she told him the real horror of what her life had become. She told him everything even up to the point where in the last thirty minutes or so she had been forced to have sex with five different men in the back of the mobile brothel.

"I want to stay here with you, please."

Pablo knew it was too dangerous; the pimps looked like more trouble than he could handle and were probably carrying weapons. "Look you need to go with them."

She hugged him again. "No… no!"

"Conchita… you must, but I will get help. I will call the police… promise."

As soon as Conchita left with the pimp, Pablo called the Collier County Sheriff's Office and told them what he just witnessed. The Community Policing Officer at the Golden Gate substation called my Supervisor for assistance, and then I was called to respond. I just recently returned to work after a very complicated birth with my fourth child, D.J. I had spent time away from the office recovering and now I was back and raring to go.

After I got the call, my husband came home to stay with the kids, and I headed to the office. Everyone involved at the station was debriefed; the FBI, undercover police, patrol division, criminal detectives and me, as the victim's advocate. Conchita had told her old school friend how she was being transported around the area that night in a mobile brothel to different locations to meet with potential customers.

We drove to our command area and waited on a side street for any updates about the whereabouts of the van. The Command Center was in the parking lot of the vocational school on Airport Pulling Road. I sat in the passenger seat next to the FBI agent. Probably for the first time in my life, I just sat in silence.

Around midnight we got a message that the white van was stopped not far away.

"Ok, let's go," the FBI agent winked at me. "Buckle up, Anna, just in case."

I've never put a seat belt on so fast in my life.

A minute later, with lights flashing and sirens wailing, our car pulled out on the main road, my knuckles white from holding onto the seat belt and my heart beating so fast in my chest I thought I was going to collapse.

Up ahead of us, I could see another police car, the white van stopped in front of it. Our car stopped about twenty yards behind it.

"Stay in here, Anna," the FBI agents instructed me. To be truthful I was more than pleased to just sit there and observe. Jumping out and becoming a hero, or a dead hero, was something I try to avoid.

Two short, chubby Hispanic men stood motionless, hands above their heads, near the unmarked FBI car. Within seconds they were handcuffed, read their rights and put into a car. Another officer opened up the back doors of the van. The FBI agent motioned for me to come over.

"Everyone out," I heard him say as I approached. Six girls piled out, looking quite shook up from the car chase. They lined up against the wall, hands over their heads.

"What's going on?" one of them asked.

Her question was ignored. She turned her attention to me, glaring at me up and down. "What are you looking at?" she hissed.

I too ignored her question.

The girls appeared to be from seventeen to twenty-five and of Latin decent and didn't look at all like what I expected. Most wore jeans, had new shoes on, and they smelled clean.

Two of the younger girls looked and acted quite differently than the others.

They stood together, looking very scared and were both sobbing. They weren't talking back like the others; they just stood there quiet, very timid.

All the girls were loaded back into the van with me to be transported back to our office in Naples to start the interviews. The two male suspects were retained by the FBI and taken to another station.

The girls sat in the back, quiet at first. We drove on Airport Pulling Road towards the station. Suddenly the noise of another police siren rose up behind us. I glanced in the mirror and saw a cop car flashing for us to pull over.

"What the ...." the FBI agent gestured when he saw the car. He pulled over and waited for the police officer to appear.

"Put both your hands outside the window," the police officer shouted at the driver.

"I can't believe this," the FBI officer hissed, as he put his badge in one of his hands and followed the order. The deputy came to the driver's side, shining his flashlight in to our vehicle. Suddenly he saw me. "Hi, Anna," he said, "What are you doing?"

I could feel the girls glaring at me from behind.

"We've rescued these girls," I replied. "The driver is an FBI agent and we're on our way to the office to interview them all about a potential human trafficking case."

He looked at the girls, then at me, then at the FBI agent who by now was pretty mad. "Sorry... sorry!" the policeman apologized, "I didn't know... you were speeding... so I was just... just carrying out my duty.... carry on... sorry ...sorry, Anna."

We drove off.

"Thanks for saving me from a traffic citation," the FBI agent joked.

It broke the ice with the girls. "Well, well," one of the older girls shouted from the back. "I never thought I'd see a Fed being out done by a regular traffic cop."

They all sat there giggling, except for the two girls, while the FBI agent got redder and redder.

"It wasn't his fault," he objected, "This car doesn't have a law enforcement special tag so he wouldn't have known."

They all laughed again, only louder. I giggled to myself as well.

When everything settled back down, I overheard one of the girls reminding the others to keep their stories straight so they didn't get beat when they were released. She told the other girls not to talk with or cooperate with the police. She said that if they did, she would know and tell the guys as soon as they were released from jail. She must not have realized I could understand Spanish.

I later found out she was the "bottom" as they are called in the business. The "bottom" is the lead or caretaker of the girls, the one who has gained the traffickers' trust in return for a little more freedom. She is often used to instill fear amongst the other girls and recruit new girls for the business.

It's a well-used tactic. The pimps always use emotional manipulation by favoring one girl over the others. This frequently changes. It helps establish a hierarchy within the "stable" to ensure constant competition for rewards and promotions to the girl who produces the most money.

This bottom was probably the oldest and seemed the most street-wise out of the group.

By the time we got to the office, the restaurants were closed so I bought snacks and soda from the vending machines for the girls. I always kept some change in the drawer of my desk, just for this purpose. They thanked me, and sat in one line eating their food.

Along with another FBI agent, we started interviewing each girl in turn. The bottom was first. She didn't tell us much. She said she wasn't being held against her will by the men and stated she loved doing it. In fact, she was getting ready to go on her own because she knew she could make more money. She showed us her business card. It simply said, *Carne Fresca* with her cell phone number. She was already planning to take these girls with her when she struck out into the business on her own.

Next, was one of the girls. She was seventeen. She told me she was married to one of the pimps who had been arrested and her role was to stay at home to cook and clean as a good wife. She stated that he would never force her or ask her to have sex with anyone else except him.

Then Conchita walked in very slowly, eyes fixed on the ground. She didn't answer any question I asked. She just shook her head yes or no. She would glance at the FBI agent and then quickly stare at the ground again. This went on for about ten minutes. I asked the FBI agent to get us some water; he was smart enough to realize what I was up to.

"Look, Conchita," I said. "There's nothing to be afraid of. No one's going to hurt you… I promise."

She looked at the door, then back at me. "I've been warned not to talk to the police."

"Please… you will be fine. I'm not the police… I promise."

She looked at me. "Please, Anna… I want to go home… I don't want to do this or live like this. Please help me and my friend Theresa." She grabbed my hand. I told her that I would help her but that I needed her to give me some information so we could charge Javier and his accomplice. In doing so, she could help us make sure that Javier could be sent to prison and would not be able to do this to other girls. Conchita cried. Then she agreed to give me some information. Over the next hour she told me all about her kidnapping and horrific life.

Conchita told me that after she crossed the border, she was taken to Phoenix, Arizona. She said when she arrived in Phoenix, she was sold to another trafficker. She and Theresa were taken in vans first to Mesa, Arizona, and then all the way to Fort Myers. They were given to Javier. Before they started turning tricks for Javier, they went sightseeing. They went to New York, Washington, DC, Orlando and Key West

We later found pictures of the girls standing in front of the Statue of Liberty, the White House, the Lincoln Memorial, with Mickey Mouse at Disney World, and in Key West. The traffickers spent a couple of weeks just traveling with the girls and taking pictures of them everywhere they went. After the trip, the girls were returned to Fort Myers. They were now told that they would have to turn tricks to compensate for the sightseeing trip they had just been on.

The traffickers also would constantly remind the girls that they were "illegals" and if they were caught by law enforcement, they would be taken to a detention camp. They told them that the detention center was a place where the guards would rape the foreign detainees.

Conchita did not want to share much information about her life in Mexico or her family. She was ashamed and afraid that her family would find out that she had been forced into working as a prostitute and not as a waitress. As a way to keep Conchita in line and to stop her from running away, the traffickers had made a video tape of her having sex. They told her that if she didn't do the things that they told her to do, or if she tried to escape, they would bring the tape to Mexico to show her family what she was doing in Florida.

We finished conducting the rest of the interviews around ten the next morning. It had been a long Friday night. I was exhausted, mentally drained, but so pleased because Conchita and Theresa had been rescued. The other four girls openly denied being held against their will. In fact most were upset because they had been arrested. The other girls where in the process of going independent and on their own to make better money and not share the profits with the suspects.

"The men were only protecting us," one girl commented. "I've been working as a prostitute since I was a teenager living in Mexico and I love having sex. It's what I do well."

The four were detained since they had no legal status. They were transported to the Collier County Jail until immigration officers could transport them to the detention facility in Miami.

We had no resources to place Conchita and Theresa at a safe shelter. I called the local domestic violence shelter and was told that they only took domestic violence victims. I put the phone down and called everywhere I could think of, until I finally found a homeless shelter that agreed to take them for a short period of time.

The two victims were advised of their rights and were transported to the homeless shelter in Immokalee until we could find a better shelter for them to receive the services they needed. The shelter said they would provide them with clothing and food. I told the girls to get some sleep and reminded them they were safe and I would come see them the next day.

I'd been awake for twenty-five hours straight by now and was exhausted. I kissed my baby and my husband, and then I went to sleep for a short time. When I woke up, I quickly fed my baby and then called the shelter. The lady there told me the two girls were doing just fine. They had eaten a good meal, had a shower and had gone back to sleep.

The next morning I called the shelter again to see how the girls were.

"They're doing just fine," the woman told me.

I felt relived. "Great… can I speak to one of them please?"

"Um… we gave them some money," the woman hesitated. "They've gone out to get some Mexican food."

"What?" Something didn't sound right.

"Yes… they won't be long." Again she didn't sound convincing.

"How long will they be? I'm supposed to be coming over with the FBI agent… we need to see them."

"Take your time… they're fine." She hung up.
Something was nagging at me. An hour later I called back.

"Sorry but they're still not back," the same woman explained again. Now I was really suspicious. "Look I need to speak with one of the girls urgently."

"They won't be long…."

I confronted her. "What's going on? Where are Conchita and Theresa?" I demanded to know.

There was silence on the other end. "I'm sorry," she blurted out. "So sorry… we feel so bad."

"Where are they?" I almost screamed down the receiver. "Has anyone taken them?"

"No… no… it's just that we all felt so bad for what happened to the girls that we all chipped in and bought them bus tickets to go back to Mexico... we were only trying to help them."

I hung up the phone and called the FBI. An agent called the border patrol but was advised the bus had gone through the border a few hours before. All the work of so many people was almost completely wasted. The FBI had built a beautiful case, with good evidence. We had two excellent witnesses. They were gone. The FBI lost the human trafficking charge and could only charge the suspects with harboring illegals for profit and transporting illegals. It was frustrating for the FBI agent and for me.

About a month later, the federal prosecutor based in DC called to tell me his partner wanted to reinterview the five girls who were being held at the Charlotte County Jail and they needed my assistance to translate and make the girls feel comfortable with a familiar face. I made arrangements with my son, Rob, to go with me to the meeting at the Charlotte County Jail to help take care of his baby brother while I was assisting the prosecutors.

The corrections officers at the jail were super nice. They helped my son take care of his baby brother… even to change his diaper! During the interview, the girls had the same attitude as before.

"Javier" was actually Leopoldo Velasquez. He and his accomplice, Angel Ambriz-Rojas, were sentenced to two years in federal prison and deported after the sentence was over. The other four women with Velasquez and Ambriz-Rojas were detained as witnesses and deported after the two men were sentenced.

The experience helped me realize that getting the victims out of their situations was not going to be enough. I needed a place they could feel safe and secure until their traffickers could be brought to justice.

I also realized that I needed to educate and train anyone that would have first-hand contact with potential trafficking victims. This included the police who had a hard time seeing them as anything other than prostitutes. One police officer later confessed to me that every time he arrested a prostitute, the last thing he thought about were victims; to him they were criminals and deserved to go to jail.

Thanks Mister President

My work as a victim's advocate led me to my involvement in the fight against human trafficking, but it was my interest in law enforcement that got it all started.

That began when my family first moved to Naples. My favorite TV show was *Cops*, and I was a faithful viewer. After my second daughter was born, I attended a Children Services Council meeting with my husband and met Sheriff Don Hunter. His presentation impressed me so much that I joined the six-week course known as the Sheriff's Citizens Academy. I signed up for all the Advanced Citizen Academies (there were seven in all) and was hooked. Part of the program was an opportunity to ride-along with an officer. I knew that the two major areas where there were a lot of migrants were East Naples and Immokalee. I did my two squad car ride-alongs in each of these areas, on the four p.m. to two a.m. shift, and I noticed there were hardly any Hispanic officers. I ended up doing a lot of translating.

I was amazed with all the work and responsibilities that a police officer faces on a daily basis. And since I could see the need, I volunteered at nights as a translator in Immokalee.

I would drive to Immokalee on a Friday or Saturday afternoon to join the afternoon shift and not return back home until two or three in the morning. If needed, I would assist the officers with translations. A lot of the detectives liked it when I translated for them because I always translated what was said word for word. A lot of translators just summarize what was said and sometimes the meaning gets lost.

I was careful not to side with the people just because we both were Hispanic. I always thought that the law is the law and if you do something wrong, you have to suffer the consequences.

It was hard and often intense work, but I loved every minute of it. It was a new world for me. I got involved with helping the community with various awareness and education programs mainly concerning subjects regarding domestic violence, victim rights and translations.

I was appointed by the Board of County Commission of Collier County to the Hispanic Affairs Advisory Board and was later elected Chairperson.

When my daughter turned two years old, I decided to go back to work. A dear friend recommended me for a position at a domestic violence shelter. Most of the work was based in Immokalee, which meant I was able to continue helping the people of the town with translating.

I started doing more presentations about domestic violence to the migrant community around Immokalee and kept volunteering with the sheriff's office. Since we had developed a great working relationship, the officers would refer me cases on a daily basis. I was even allowed to move my office into the sheriff's office where I could work side by side with the domestic violence detective.

In September of 1995, I got a call from the captain of the Criminal Investigation Division. He said he was impressed with my work and that he wanted to offer me a full-time position with the sheriff's office as a victim advocate. The starting salary was more than I was earning, plus I would be paid for overtime and have a company car. I accepted the position eagerly.

My role was varied. I would assist with transportation, victim rights, court advocacy, crisis intervention, death notification, funeral assistance, and community presentations. I dealt with cases of sexual abuse and domestic violence in and around Collier Country, Florida.

I did translations with victims and witnesses, but the Collier County detectives trusted me enough to translate for them during interrogations, too. One particular case was especially difficult for me to translate. The Sheriff's Department had received a complaint that man who ran an ice cream truck was giving ice cream to the young girls in exchange for sex. It was an old man, not thirty or forty, but in his late seventies. The interview room was small, a table and two chairs. The detective and the suspect sat in the chairs with the table between them. There was not even enough space in the room for another chair, so I had to sit on the floor. When the elderly man started talking about his private part it made me feel very uncomfortable, but I continued to do the translation. The man eventually pled guilty to the crimes, so thankfully, I never had to testify in court on that case.

I worked in close quarters with Lieutenant Will, a detective in the property crimes division. I encouraged him to apply for the Domestic Violence Detective position as I felt he would be a great asset to the unit.

He did and was appointed to the unit. Our desks were face to face. A year later the Victim Assistance Unit Supervisor resigned, and I felt that a sworn officer should be in charge of the unit so that victim advocates would be respected and consider more than "tree huggers" as some deputies referred to us. Again I encouraged Lieutenant Will to consider the position. He did apply and got the job! I believed we made a great team but later realized he had his own agenda—promotions.

The problem was that Lieutenant Will was a great detective but had no idea what victim advocates did. He knew the investigative side, but he didn't know the nurturing part. He shadowed me on the ride to learn what I did.

Lieutenant Will often picked my brain for ideas. "I know we respond to this type of case," he said. "What kind of needs are we missing?"

I told him, for example, when they had tourists who were victims of robbery and were left with no money, maybe they could create a program, get gift cards donated and provide these victims with the cards. I shared great some great ideas for new services and programs for our unit. Then I would later hear someone talk about what great ideas Lieutenant Will had. And they sounded awfully familiar.

I was also getting referrals and requests to help FBI special agents with human trafficking cases. These were considered outside of my duties that were funded by the Victims of Crime Act for the State of Florida. I was allowed to assist in these cases but did not get paid. So I did my normal victim advocacy work for Collier County and shuffled my schedule to do human rights cases on my own time, a lot of it at the request of other agencies such as the FBI.

I still reported to Lieutenant Will's office, telling him about the latest case that I was working with the FBI. I would bring my files to show him. Lieutenant Will would return the file and say keep doing what you're doing but make sure that you don't put in an overtime card because this is not part of duty of the Sheriff's Office. That's a federal crime. But you can help them on your own time!

The more I uncovered, the more it drove me to do my best to make a difference, to change as many lives as I could.

Things at work were going well. I became more and more involved in human trafficking and was earning a reputation as somewhat of an expert. Then in the early part of 2002, after my trip to DC to witness the signing of the T1 visa bill Lieutenant Will was suddenly interested in what I was doing.

He hadn't really been interested in human trafficking; He said human trafficking was a federal crime and not a state issue. But now he was drilling me with questions and he requested all of my files on the Tecum case. I was tickled to see his sudden interest. With pleasure, I gave him all the information without asking any questions. He didn't know anything about the cases because he hadn't been involved at all, but I just assumed he was at last paying attention.

I had a very difficult pregnancy with my son D.J. and was hospitalized for three months due to pre-term labor. After my son was born, a month prior to his due date, I had to stay home with him some extra time. Lieutenant Will kept calling my house asking me for details regarding the human trafficking cases that I worked. He stated that he was working on a project and a possible grant position so I would be assigned to a human trafficking pilot program. I provided him the information he requested. Lieutenant Will couldn't get to my files on Human Trafficking because the filing cabinets were locked and since these files were not part of the Sheriff Office records, I had a lot of them at home where I was completing the paperwork and doing the follow-up.

Then the Blackjack case came up and Lieutenant Will left me in charge. He had no interest in staying involved.

Throughout my maternity leave, Lieutenant. Will called with all kinds of questions about the Tecum case.

When I returned to work, I made arrangements to work the evening shift so I could stay with D.J. during the day and my husband could take care of him at night. I was working from four thirty in the afternoon until two in the morning, or even later if I got called out to provide assistance to a victim or translation to a Deputy.

I settled in at work one afternoon and checked my email, as usual, expecting the same mundane messages. Then I saw one that caught my eye. I couldn't believe what I was reading. I stared in amazement as I read the general invitation to all staff in the department to join our supervisor the following Thursday at the training center as Lieutenant Will was getting presented with a state award for his initiative in the investigation and victim advocacy to victims of human trafficking. I read it again, looking for my name as well. There was no mention of me at all, nothing. I had been completely overlooked.

I have never been an attention seeker. I believe God had given me a purpose in life and I don't need awards or recognition. But to give recognition to Lieutenant Will, who was not even involved in the cases, felt like the biggest slap in the face I had ever experienced. Everyone at the office knew it. When a detective read the notice on the computer, he said, "What a son of a bitch!"

I was shocked, heartbroken and deeply hurt. I had been stabbed in the back. And although I had never really been able to figure him out, I would have never imagined he would stoop to something so low.

I couldn't even look at him. Colleagues tried to apologize for the injustice. I tried to keep calm, but eventually I broke down right there in my own office, crying like a baby. I was so upset, I couldn't speak to anyone. I called my husband in tears and explained what had happened. He asked me to please take the day off and come home immediately.

When I got home, my initial disappointment and shock quickly turned to anger. I felt so betrayed. As usual, my husband was very supportive.

"Quit," he said.

"What?"

"Just quit. You don't need them."

"But what am I going to do? We have four children to support."

"Do it yourself. Go rescue victims. I'll support and help you," he replied.

"I can't do that," I hesitated. "I just can't."

"Why not?"

That night I started to think about it. "Why not?" Maybe my husband was right and the actions of my boss were just the push I needed to go and pursue my passion. I had been a victim's advocate for ten years. Now it was time to devote all my time to working against human trafficking.

This was a turning point in my life, and it was up to me to decide my future. That night I wrote my letter of resignation giving my two weeks' notice. When I handed it in, everyone in the department appeared stunned. They asked me to stay. Even my boss promised me things would be different. However it was too late. My mind was made up.

In April 2004, I left the sheriff's office to start a new life, a life focused on saving children and adults across America.

I am grateful to former Sheriff Don Hunter and the Collier County Sheriff's Office for giving me the opportunity to serve the citizens of Collier County. I also received a certificate from the Federal Bureau of Investigations in recognition for my "outstanding assistance" to the FBI in connection with their investigative efforts in the Tecum Case, the Black Jack case and Alicia's case, all cases I worked with the sheriff's office.

On May 17, 2004, the Immigrant Rights Advocacy Centre, Inc. was born, and a month later Florida Coalition against Human Trafficking (FCAHT) was founded. My husband dipped into the little savings we had left and paid for the registration of the non-profit corporation. He surprised me by ordering my first business cards, getting my first computer, and buying me a fifty-dollar used desk he bought at the Habitat for Humanity thrift store. And he leased an office space with my first phone number. I was thrilled! It was a new beginning for me; I couldn't wait to get started.

My husband, Frank Rodriguez, is a quiet man with lots of energy. He has been very active with issues affecting the minority community of Collier County. A lot of my success is due to his unwavering support. Frank has told me, "If you only save one life, it's worth the effort."

Frank would like to attend more public events to show support for my work, but he has stayed home to watch our children. He is a backstage kind of person.

My office, based in Golden Gate City, Naples, wasn't a big workspace, just enough room for me, a desk, filing cabinet and telephone. I didn't care how small it was. It was mine! I made a sort of business plan, the vision of what I wanted to do.

After the mishap with the mobile brothel case, I knew the first thing I had to do was make sure I had emergency housing with well-trained counselors on hand to help victims deal with the emotional burden of their situation. And I had to ensure that they were kept safe from persistent traffickers looking to reclaim their merchandise. As I had seen, existing community service providers just weren't equipped to deal with these special cases.

Training was also a priority. I needed to get the community on the same page; I had to educate law enforcement agencies, medical facilities, faith-based groups, and civil and community organizations to bring awareness about victims and recognition of the indicators of human trafficking.

I started off by contacting other agencies and people I knew from my victim advocate days, by phone and email, to advise them of my new contact number and what I was doing. They were all very excited and supportive.

I made contact with the Federal Bureau of Investigation, the Immigration and Customs Enforcement and various county sheriff's offices and police departments in the state.

Although tough and very different from having the security of the sheriff's office to back me, it was one of the most memorable and enjoyable times of my life. There were no territorial wars. There was no competition. Nobody really knew what human trafficking was all about and although my knowledge on the subject wasn't great, I was a few steps ahead of anyone else.

Financing proved to be my biggest challenge. I was on my own with no salary, and I had yet to do any fundraising. My family was very supportive, and the experience brought my husband and me closer than ever, but we had to make some drastic financial adjustments. Meals out were limited. We sold some things and cut back on the smallest of luxuries in life like new cars and home improvements. Although my kids didn't fully understand, they didn't complain.

I never thought for one minute that at my age I would end up doing anything like this, and with such passion, commitment and drive. I didn't really have time to wonder "why me" or if I was completely insane. I imagined there were, and probably still are, lots of people in the world much better equipped to help save God's children from a lifetime of misery. Yet whatever God's reason behind selecting me, I was just so happy and privileged to be able to do my bit to help. These were my children, too, and I was determined do everything in my power to rescue them and bring their evil adductors to justice.

My first day, I felt like a new woman, a woman on a mission, a mission to save as many children as physically and mentally possible.

Nothing was going to stop me.

After a slow first few days, things started to snowball. It didn't take long for my name and my new role to get around, and I was soon asked to set up speaking engagements for various groups at various events. God was definitely on my side. Then one phone call took me by complete surprise.

"Hello, Anna Rodriguez," a woman's voice spoke. "I'm helping to organize the first ever Human Trafficking National Conference in Tampa and we would like you to speak at the event."

"Oh," I replied, "that will be wonderful." I replied, quickly checking my empty calendar.

"Great, we would like you to open the entire conference with Deputy Rick Castro from the San Diego Sheriff's Office."

"Oh!"

Then he added, "The President of the United States, George W. Bush, will be there along with some of the most powerful people from all over the country. So it's going to be quite a big and prestigious event, Mrs. Rodriguez."

I didn't know what to say. I had to pinch myself to make sure I had heard the man on the other end right. "So you want me to speak at a conference in front of the President of the United States?" I quietly muttered back.

"Yes ma'am, and also the Attorney General and the Governor of Florida."

"Wow!"

I called my husband immediately to tell him the news.

"Go girl… you deserve it," he yelled down the phone. "You really are a hero," he added.

"Don't talk stupid. I haven't done anything special." I didn't just say that. I believed it. I was in the right place at the right time, and any decent law-abiding person would have done what I did."

It was an exciting but anxious time. Frank tried to keep me calm, but since I don't drink or smoke, I resorted to talking non-stop to calm my nerves.

Several days before the event, I received a phone call from a man who wrote many of the speeches for the President. He wanted to check some details with me and make sure everything was perfect.

It was all moving so fast.

The day before the event, Frank and I, along with baby D.J., arrived at the Marriot Hotel at Channelside in Tampa. The day seemed hotter than normal, or maybe my nerves just made me intolerant to the normal Florida heat. As we walked in to the reception, my legs turned to jelly. Secret service personnel were all over the place. I suddenly realized what a big deal this really was.

That night I couldn't sleep. Especially after I found out that I was going to be speaking to five hundred guests. Never in my life had I spoken to so many people and to so many distinguished guests including the President of the United States of America. It was like the night before Christmas and all of my birthdays rolled up into one special moment.

When I did eventually nod off, I kept waking up every hour looking at the clock, terrified I would oversleep. Finally at six in the morning, I couldn't take it anymore. I got up to start getting ready for the big day. Frank's pleas for me to just come back to bed fell on deaf ears. I couldn't keep still, never mind go back to sleep. My hands were slick and cold as clams. My heart pumped faster than a Ricky Martin beat. I couldn't eat breakfast. I could barely hold a glass of water, my hands were shaking so badly.

Downstairs seemed more manic than the day before. Even more secret security personnel lined up in every corridor, standing tall by every door. I waited in line to get checked through security before getting into the main conference room. Sadly Frank hadn't been invited. He waited in the room upstairs.

Inside the hall, people had already arrived and the room was almost full. There was a swarm of media setting up their equipment in the back, bright lights were already fixed on the stage.

"Mrs. Rodriguez." I was greeted by one of the Department of Justice organizers. He took me to the back of the stage. As we walked through the mass of people, he off-loaded a list of instructions of what to do and what not to do. Someone else strapped a wireless microphone on me. "After you come off stage, meet me back at this location," the man said. He added that first I would meet with Attorney General Ashcroft and then go with him to the room to meet the President of the United States and his brother, Jeb Bush, who was at that time the Governor of the State of Florida.

There was no time to panic. Suddenly, I was walking on a stage that went on forever. I thought I was going to faint, honestly, pass-out right there in front of everyone on my big day.

Luckily I held it together and once I started my speech, my nerves calmed down and the butterflies flapping around in the pit of my stomach took a short nap. In fact I began to enjoy it. It was empowering exposing what was really going on in right in our own back yard. I answered a few questions regarding my experience working my first human trafficking case which became a US landmark case. As soon as I finished my presentation, I was rushed back stage to get ready to meet the President.

Now the nerves really kicked in and the butterflies woke up. I stood, waiting in line with many important people. There was Attorney General Ashcroft, then Ms. Deborah Daniels who was the Assistant Attorney General. Then there was Mr. Paul Perez, the former US Attorney Middle District of Florida, and then little old Anna. I felt so out of place as I stood quietly watching and admiring the whole protocol surrounding the arrival of the President. It ran like a machine—everyone knew exactly what to do and where to stand. The Secret Service officers merged into the background.

I didn't have to long to wait. A small commotion rose up to my left. The President entered the room. I watched him, my eyes drawn to his every movement. He smiled, he nodded at certain people and then unbelievably he came straight over to me. "Anna Rodriguez," he said, "I'm so impressed. I've been reading about you while coming here on Air Force One." I stood there, dumb with mouth open. "Thanks for the great work you are doing," he added. He shook my hand, and a man appeared to take our picture.

Next his brother, Jeb Bush, the Governor of Florida shook my hand and also thanked me for my work. Then President Bush's daughter did the same.

The President stood by my side, relaxed and cool. "Come on guys," he joked and winked at me, "Let's get this show on the road."

Along with the others I was led onto the stage before the President appeared to great applause. I sat on the far right side of the room next to

Paul Perez and the Sheriff of Manatee County.

I still couldn't believe I was there. Me! Little Anna Rodriguez, mother of four, on the same stage as the President of the United States, George W. Bush. Maybe it was all some big mistake; perhaps I'd gotten someone else's invitation in the mail. But here I was, an emotional wreck sitting in the auditorium in the conference center in Tampa, looking out at five hundred faces and a mass of TV cameras.

I glanced across to my right. US Attorney General John Ashcroft, whom I had met before during the Chica case, turned and smiled at me. I smiled back. Too overwhelmed to speak, I sat sobbing and couldn't concentrate on what the President said as his voice boomed through the sound system. Suddenly I heard my name as clear as day ringing out around the auditorium.

"Anna Rodriguez, where are you? Stand up?'"

My heart skipped a beat. It was the President; he was calling out to me, motioning me from the front of the podium where he stood.

Every eye in the place shifted across to stare directly at me. I could feel the lights of the TV cameras light up my face. I didn't know what to do, so I just sat there.

"Anna, he's calling your name. Stand up," Paul Perez whispered next to me.

I tried to move, but my legs wouldn't work. Slowly I got to my feet, my face red as a tomato, tears of joys raced down my cheeks. I waved back at him.

"Thanks for coming, Anna," President Bush said, turning back to face the audience. I slumped down in my seat, pleased to be out of the glare.

He continued with his address. "All the steps I've outlined today are important, yet, the success will depend on the courage of individuals, people like Anna. She is a victim advocate. I think you might have met her earlier today. A few years ago, Anna was working for the Collier Country Sheriff's Department when she was called to what appeared to be a routine domestic violence call. Upon arriving at the scene, she noticed a nineteen-year-old woman named Chica crying quietly in the corner of the apartment. After some coaxing, Chica told Anna her story."

He went on to tell them all about how Chica had been kidnapped from her family in Guatemala and smuggled into the United States, kept as a slave and forced to work without pay in the tomato fields of central Florida and then raped at night.

I could hear the loud gasp from members of the audience. One woman at the front put her hands over her face in disbelief.

The President's voice rose a notch. "Anna was told by her superiors there was nothing she could do for Chica except turn her case over to the INS. She didn't give up. Anna Rodriguez has a huge heart. Thanks to her persistence, Chica was rescued and her captor is now in prison." He purposely left a pause.

The sudden applause overwhelmed me as tears continued to fall. I couldn't quit crying; not just for me and my happiness, but also for Chica, for the thousands of others like her. Some people rose to their feet and cheered. The President's outstretched arms brought quiet back to the room. He finished his speech by thanking everyone. I stood and clapped as he walked to the front of the stage to shake hands with some of the people in the front row.

I watched in awe. Then as he was leaving, he approached me again. I stood there holding my breath as he got nearer and nearer.

"Keep up the good work, Anna. You are my hero," he whispered. "There should be more Anna Rodriguezes across America." He winked at me again before disappearing amongst a throng of people and the Secret Service.

I slumped back down in my seat, stunned, watching the crowd file into the foyer. A dark-haired woman came over shook my hand and thanked me for being such an inspiration.

She hugged me.

We walked together towards the big wooden doors. People stopped to shake my hand, thanking me for my efforts. Outside the room, an army of reporters swarmed around me, shoving their microphones into my face. All the major networks wanted to talk to me, wanted to know *my* story.

I met all of them in turn, answering question after question. It took forever, but to be honest, I didn't mind. While the rest of the delegates were preparing to sit down for lunch, I was still on the media merry-go-around, still telling the world about what was really going on in our country. In the end, US Attorney General John Ashcroft's assistant came looking for me and dragged me away. She informed me that Mr. Ashcroft wanted me to sit with him for lunch. We walked silently along the corridor.

"Excuse me," I said to her, "'There's something I really need to do." She stopped. "My husband... he's upstairs with my baby. Do you mind if I just said a quick hello? It won't take long."

She glanced at her watch and smiled. "Okay. I don't think another five minutes will hurt."

Floating on air, I rushed back as fast as I could to our room.

"I saw it all on the TV," my husband wrapped his arms around me. We hugged each other tightly. "I'm so proud of you... we both are." He nodded to where my eleven-month-old son was sound asleep on the bed in the next room. "You deserve it. You were only acting as a mother protecting her own child."

He kissed me, and then the wave of emotion engulfed me. I burst out crying again, and then my husband started, which made me cry even more. We held each other close in our posh hotel room. I knew I wouldn't have been here if it wasn't for him. He was and still is my rock.

"Quick, you better go back," he said.

I rushed to the bathroom to freshen up. With tears still rolling down my face, I stared at myself in the mirror. I still couldn't believe that less than an hour ago the most powerful man on the planet was holding me in such high esteem.

I knew at that moment more than ever before that this was my calling. The Lord had given me this purpose in life—to rescue His children and to breathe hope and happiness back into their lives.

My parents back in Miami would have been so proud of what I achieved. My father in particular spent a large part of his life living, or as he put it, surviving, in a suburb of New York City where at the age of five months, he suffered polio that left him disabled. He had a tough life growing up—a hard uncompromising upbringing where he was often teased and bullied by other children. Yet he was a survivor, never afraid to push himself and challenge his disability, always trying to prove people wrong. Maybe that's where my drive and spirit came from.

"Anna, you better get back downstairs," my husband tapped on the bathroom door.

I wiped my eyes and went back into the room. Minutes later I took my place next to Attorney General John Ashcroft. With the serious pressure behind me, I was suddenly hungry. We talked through most of the meal. He was wonderful and very interested to find out all about the coalition and my family. I had a great lunch.

The rest of the conference was amazing as well. People stopped me to congratulate me for being recognized by the President; I could relax a bit more and just enjoy the rest of the event.

The Mark of the Devils

Once I got back from the conference in Tampa, I started getting speaking requests from all over the nation. I travelled far and wide from Philadelphia to St. Louis, from New York to California and everywhere in between. I survived on a shoe string budget, with no funding and no staff to help me. People thought I was leading a glamorous life with all the travel, yet in fact I was more like the director of a one man band, and I was playing all the instruments, driving the tour bus and standing outside in the rain trying to sell the T-shirts. Our life savings began to erode daily as I paid for some of my expenses like taxis, meals, gas for my car and hotel accommodations when not covered by the agency who had invited me to speak.

I soldiered on, determined not to give in, money or not. This was what I signed up for, what God had called me to do, and I knew it wasn't going to be easy. The most important thing for me was that all of a sudden I became known as Anna Rodriguez, the founder and CEO of the Florida Coalition against Human Trafficking, the woman who fought against the traffickers. One police officer politely said I was the "lady with the balls to challenge the evil of trafficking."

However, pretty soon the wrong kind of attention came knocking on my door, something I naively never expected.

One morning I sat in my small office putting together the finishing touches on a presentation for later that week. I had just reached the last slide when the phone rang.

"Good morning, Anna Rodriguez speaking," I chirruped.

Silence.

"Hello," I said again.

Again nothing. I was just about to hang up when I heard someone breathing on the other end.

"Who's there?"

A man spoke slowly and concisely. "Stop what you're doing," his chilling voice crept down the line and crawled into my ear like a spider. "Stop it, if you want to see your kids grow up."

I dropped the phone, staring at it as it dangled from the top of the desk. I reached over and slammed it back on the receiver before letting out a scream.

My heart beat fast, the room spun around and around.

I panicked.

"My kids, my husband," the words echoed around my head.

I raced out of the office, not bothering to lock up. I drove home, tears rolling down my face, fearing the worse.

My husband could tell something was wrong as soon as I rushed through the gate into the back yard where he and the kids were playing.

"Hey, looks like you've seen a ghost," he joked.

I couldn't reply. I hugged them all, one by one. It took me a while until I could tell him what had happened.

I didn't want this for my family; I didn't want them to live in fear because of me.

For the first time since it had all begun, my husband didn't say anything. He just held me tight.

Later as I lay in bed, the image of Chica's face popped into my mind. I remembered how sad she looked and how different she looked now, full of life, full of hope. I knew that I couldn't just quit because someone had scared me. There were others depending on me to help them. I then realized that quitting and walking away was just what whoever had called wanted me to do; they wanted me to run away and hide, disappear so they could continue doing what they did. I began to think that maybe they were the ones now running scared and it boosted my confidence once again.

Later that night I woke my husband up to tell him the news, "I'm carrying on, if it's okay with you."

"Of course it is," he nodded.

I couldn't sleep; I just stared at the ceiling until the sun came up.

I went back to my office the following morning, but that one phone call changed my outlook. I became more cautious, a little paranoid of everyone I met and everywhere I went. I started imagining I was being followed, my family being watched. I couldn't sit in a restaurant without feeling eyes staring at me, perhaps waiting for the right moment to strike. It was a stressful time.

Then another victim, Angie, was identified, thanks to the staff at North Collier Hospital. I had done some training at the hospital a few months prior for the social workers and emergency personal. So they knew how to recognize a human trafficking victim. Angie's abuser was in the hospital too. The staff separated him and interviewed her alone. Angie was a fifteen- year-old girl with a nine-month-old child. Angie said that she was in fear of going back to Immokalee and kept telling staff there she was being held against her will.

It was obvious she was a potential victim of human trafficking and being used as a prostitute. I asked her to tell me about herself. She said she was from a small isolated village in Guatemala which was very close to the border with Mexico, about five hours from Huehuetenango.

Angie had a rough life. Her mother had passed away when she was young. She was living with her father but not getting along well with her father's girlfriend. Angie and the woman were always fighting. A recruiter came to the village. Angie thought that the best thing that she could do was to leave and come to America. Angie had been promised a job working in the kitchen of a restaurant. She thought this would be a good move for her family because she could send money back to Guatemala to help support her younger siblings.

Angie was smuggled into the United States, entering through Arizona. The coyote handed Angie over to another person who was supposed to take her to the restaurant. She was brought to Immokalee. Now she was told that she would not be working in a restaurant but in the fields picking tomatoes. At night she was expected to turn tricks. Angie did not want to prostitute herself. She was still a virgin. Her trafficker told that if she didn't do what he said, he was going to call Immigration and she would be sent back to Guatemala. Angie had no one to turn to, she was afraid, so she started turning the tricks.

Angie became pregnant and she felt that it was from her abuser, her trafficker. Before she started turning the tricks, she had to have sex with him. She continued to have sex with him even after she was turning the tricks. I asked her about her abuser. Angie said, "He brought me here from Guatemala," she told me. "He owns me. I must do whatever he tells me to do. I work in a factory for him in the day and have sex with him at night."

This sounded like Chica all over again. I took her and her baby boy to one of the safe shelters that I used often. While Angie was having a shower and getting changed, I picked the little baby up from the cot. He looked so cute in my arms, his eyes wide and full of life.

"Oh my, someone needs changing," I laid him back down on the bed and started to take his clothes off. "Oh my god," I recoiled in horror.

The baby had been branded with the initials CG on his back. It looked like it had been done with a hot fork. The baby could not sit up and had no upper muscle development. The back of his head was flat, not round. He was like a Raggedy Andy Doll. I had to bite my lip to keep from crying. The baby hadn't been allowed to develop like normal children, not allowed to crawl around on the floor.

While Angie worked during the day, a woman in a neighboring trailer watched the child. This woman just left him to lie in a cot all day. At night Angie always had to tend to her trafficker's sexual needs first before she could care for her baby. Some days she was not even allowed to see her son for two or three days.

"Who did this to him?" I asked Angie when she returned from the bathroom.

"He did. CG are his initials," she replied. "He did it when my son was only two weeks old. I told you he owns me and now he owns my baby. If I don't do whatever he says, he will sell my baby into the black market."

"No," I said, "He doesn't own you or your baby."

I asked the staff at the shelter for a camera to take pictures of the branding on his back by his left shoulder. I wanted to show the law enforcement. I couldn't believe it. Like a farmer brands their livestock. I later discovered many traffickers and pimps use this method to let others know the merchandise belongs to them and for the sense of power it gives them.

A word, initials or a symbol are tattooed or, like Angie and her boy, branded somewhere on the body of the victim. It's meant to be a permanent symbol that will never fade, an enduring reminder of who they belong to. A powerful message to the victim that basically says, "I own you and I will own you forever."

I didn't waste any time getting her out of the grip of this evil monster. I contacted the FBI to see if they could track down the trafficker while I found a place for Angie and her baby to stay safely.

Within a month of their rescue, Angie's baby was pushing himself all over the shelter in a walker. His head grew to be round and more normal. Angie started going to school, but then someone from the shelter noticed that she was pregnant again. They took her to the doctor and four months later, she had a baby girl.

It was interesting because this faith-based shelter was pushing her to give up her baby for adoption. And they even recommended a possible adoptive mother, a teacher they knew. The lady came to the shelter to spend time with Angie during her pregnancy.

When Angie had the baby, she realized that she could not give her baby up for adoption. The shelter staff got upset with her and started treating her differently. Angie's case manager, Maria, was very upset with what she was seeing.

Angie went through post-partum depression after her baby girl was born. When I arrived from one of my trips, I was contacted by the shelter to advise me that Angie was in a mental hospital because she had tried to commit suicide. The other girls at the shelter had said that she threatened to kill her kids and then herself. The shelter had already called the Department of Children and Families and was going to place the children in a foster home. I told them that I could take Angie's two children while she recovered. They would not hear it.

From the airport, I went straight to the hospital. When they unlocked her room, she came out in her bathrobe and when she saw me she came running and hugged me so hard we both fell to the floor.

"Please, Mom," she kept saying, "Take me with you. Take me away from here. Please, Mom, I love you."

We sat on the floor for a good thirty minutes or so until I was able to get her up and take her to a small family room. We sat down on a sofa. She sat close to me and held my hand tightly. She was crying. She laid her head down on my lap and was sobbing and sobbing. She begged, "Please take me out of here. Take me to my kids. They're saying that I said I would hurt my kids. They're lying! They're lying!"

"Look Angie, you need to stay here for a while. Just do me a favor. Answer all the questions the doctors ask you. Take all your medications and I will take you out." I stayed for almost two hours talking with her. She wouldn't let me go.

She stayed at the hospital for almost a month. I didn't tell her at the time that the shelter had refused to care for her kids and had placed them both in a foster home. I argued with the staff at the shelter, but they wouldn't budge. Angie was again being victimized by the same system that was supposed to help her. It took us almost seven months to get her kids back and get Angie back in another shelter. Even the foster mother who had the children was working against Angie, saying she was an unfit mother.

Angie's situation continued to get worse. She kept calling me nearly every night begging me to get her out of the shelter but wouldn't say why. It wasn't until she moved out that she told us they treated her like a slave.

I remember her case manager coming back to the office upset because when she went to pick Angie up from the shelter she was sitting outside with all her belongings. The staff at the shelter had just evicted her onto the street.

We set Angie up in an apartment. She was doing fine on her own. She got her GED. She learned how to drive. She had purchased a bicycle for her son, Eduardo, and a little tricycle for her daughter, Rosa. Rosa was three or four years old already. One day Rosa was riding her trike and she fell. There were neighbors outside who witnessed it. Angie took Rosa to the day care while she went to school. When she returned home, she was about to take a bus to pick up her children.

The Collier County Sheriff's Office Deputy Sheriff arrived. They never spoke to the neighbors, and they accused Angie of beating Rosa because of the prior DCF case. They arrested Angie for child abuse and took her to jail. I tried to reason with the young detective asking him to question the neighbors but he wouldn't listen. I posted Angie's bond. She had to take a parenting class. It took her nine months to get her children back. First she was victimized by her trafficker. Then she was victimized by the system.

Angie's trafficker was never found. He left the Immokalee area before the police could talk with him. Today Angie and her kids are doing very well. She is working full-time at a large retail store. She is married to a good man. She received her T1 visa and is starting her residency process.

Not long after I started working with Angie, I got another call. This time from a man. He had a South American accent and he informed me that he used to smuggle people into the United States and he had heard about me and he wanted to help. He had read about me in a Spanish publication. He was impressed with what I was doing and decided to call me. He used to be a coyote.

"Why?" I asked suspiciously. "Why do you want to talk to me?"

"I want to come clean. Please can we meet up?" he asked. "I need to talk to you."

I wasn't sure if it was trick or not, maybe a ploy to get me to lower my guard. He could sense my hesitation. "Please, nothing will happen to you."

I did not want to meet with him in my office. I suggested that we meet in a public parking lot at the Bonita Beach Road Shopping Center. I thought if something happened to me, there would be witnesses. I didn't tell my husband. Instead I called to tell him something had come up and I wouldn't be long. I crossed my fingers. I knew it was madness.

I had told the caller I would be driving a blue car and he told me he was coming with his wife and would be in a small red Nissan. I actually lied about the color of my car. I got there a little early. I parked in a different area of the parking lot than where I had told him. It was getting dark. I could see his car parked under a streetlight near the back. I didn't know what to do, to drive past and go home or stop. I wished I had been smart enough to bring someone with me like my husband or an FBI agent.

I drove past the car several times. I could make out a woman sitting in the passenger's seat, but I also knew that didn't mean it was safe. At one point the woman got out of the car and went into the store. She was pregnant. I could see that at least he was telling me the truth about bringing his wife.

I finally got the courage to stop next to his car and get out. He did the same. I apologized for having a different car, saying that at the last minute my husband took my car, so I took his.

I had prearranged to use an office at the Lee County Sheriff's Office. I asked him if this was all right. He said that if I trusted him, he would trust me.

We went in and sat down. "My wife is having a baby," he confessed, "I want God to forgive me so my baby will be healthy." His wife was sitting right there when he said this.

"Where are you from?' I asked, looking at a deep scar above his left eye.

"Guatemala. My wife is from Mexico. I met her while smuggling her here with a group of people. I fell in love with her… we've been together two years."

I was shocked and still a bit scared. The previous phone call threat had spooked me.

Without me pushing too hard, he openly told me information regarding the routes the smugglers and traffickers use to bring the people across the border. I knew it was critical information. I told him I needed to set up an appointment with the FBI so he could share the same information with them.

He told me that he would bring a group of people across the border. He would be paid by people on the other side. He would take his cut and return the remainder to someone higher up in the criminal organization. He knew that some of the people that he had crossed would be involved in prostitution and some in forced labor. He said, "I didn't really care what happened to them, as long as I got my money. I was just doing my job."

As I sat there listening to him, I was getting very angry. I wanted to just grab him and start punching him. When he talked about this, he showed no remorse. He talked about how he separated children from their parents. He talked about how the network worked. How the "merchandise" or "pieces of meat" were brought to a certain place. "Ryders" were called and the "merchandise" was brought to "safe houses" and distributed throughout the United States. The people that were doing the transporting were all either native or white Americans. They were professional people, housewives, people in law enforcement and in the military.

A few days later he agreed to meet with the FBI and offered up a significant amount of information critical to busting lucrative human trafficking rings. After that he became an informant for law enforcement.

This man also agreed to do a documentary about human trafficking. During this time, his wife went into labor and had a baby. The documentary producer and I went up to the hospital with presents. He was so touched he asked me to be the godmother of his newborn. I politely turned down his offer. It was hard for me. He had been a trafficker until recently and even though he was coming forward with information, I still thought it important to try to keep my distance. He appeared genuinely sorry for what he'd been involved in but at times he still referred to people as "merchandise" and "pieces of meat". It was just the world he had lived in for so many years.

Later, I received an e-mail from him telling me he was moving back to Mexico and he was going to open up his own restaurant. He also had another child by then and told me he still wanted to help me whenever he could. I still keep in contact with him through e-mails.

***

In September of 2004 I received a visit from some ladies from a women's civic group in Sanibel, Florida. The assistant to Congressman Porter Goss had recommended me to them as a speaker. These ladies wanted to do something to educate their civic club and asked if I would speak at their breakfast. They said that they wanted to make human trafficking a club project. The trouble was that they really had no idea what human trafficking was. They wanted to help me with fundraisers.

I left my house early in the morning to attend the seven o'clock breakfast meeting with a couple of ladies from the club. I confidently began speaking all about her human trafficking experiences and what I thought was needed to do to combat it. The audience was a very attentive, asking a lot of questions. It went on longer than I had expected.

After my presentation, a wonderful lady from the group approached me. She wanted to help me spread the word and also help me to fundraise and help with my 501c3 tax exempt application. I had submitted the application and had not heard anything back in three months. She told me that it could take four months for the approval or denial. One of the group's members was an attorney, and she said she would talk to her to see if she would help.

It sounded too good to be true! And it was. What I didn't realize was that this woman was setting me up. The woman really wanted to use my information to set up her own non-profit organization against human trafficking.

I did a Power Point presentation for them. The group then did its own presentation using information from mine. They ended up winning the Governor's Award for the presentation and their commitment to human trafficking.

In 2005, at the Unitarian Church of Fort Myers, I met a woman who was a grant writer for the Lee County Sheriff's Office. She told me that she wanted to help me find funding by writing some grants. She was amazing! Thanks to her, I got my first two grants.

The Task Force started out as a great success but started declining once personal agendas and greed for money became the priority of one member. I decided to back away because these were not my priorities or my mission. The meeting attendance dwindled from eighty early on to not more than ten. People asked me to start another group. Instead, I just backed away and continued my work.

At last some funding was coming in to help the business progress and grow. And grow it did. In a short period of time around 2005 the operation grew considerably bigger. From one small office, it grew into a main office with four part-time staff members in Bonita Springs, and offices in Tampa, Orlando, Miami and Shalimar. My small team and I conducted numerous speaking engagements every month and travelled across the state. My international travel took me to countries I never imagined I would go.

During one human trafficking community presentation, a social worker and executive director of a shelter for teen mothers came to talk to me. "I think I have someone that sounds exactly what you have been talking about," she said.

Maria, a fifteen-year-old girl from Central America had been in the shelter's care for almost a year before she told anyone what she had been through. As I listened to woman I immediately knew she needed to talk to the FBI about it. I put her in contact with an FBI agent in the room. Within two weeks, the traffickers were arrested and the victim placed at a safe location.

When the traffickers were arrested I went with two detectives from Lee County Sheriff's Office investigating the case to meet the victim for support and to advise her that the trafficker had been arrested.

I met her in a safe location and we sat in the living room and talked. When we gave her the news that the trafficker was arrested and was being charged with human trafficking, she went deadly quiet and then said, "Thanks for believing in me. I knew I was not crazy." She was so happy to hear the new and kept smiling.

Maria lived in a small village called San Miguel Acatan, northwest of Huehuetango in Guatemala near the Mexican border. A lot of the victims that came from Guatemala lived near the Mexican border. Maria had five siblings, all from different fathers. Maria's mother met this guy, named Fernando Pascual, who was nineteen years old. He was interested in Maria. He told the mother that he was going to the United States, so Maria's mother sold Maria to Fernando for 2,000 quetzales (or about 260 US dollars.) Maria's grandmother was also living with her family and was very upset about what Maria's mother did. Maria was only eleven years of age at the time.

The story got worse. The girl sat and cried as she told me how the man had raped her not long after she was in his custody, first in Guatemala, then many times later when they had arrived in the United States.

When interviewed, Maria's mother denied selling her. Their story was of two young people falling in love. She said their daughter and Pascual had fallen in love when he started sleeping in their shack. The two shared a bed and became very close. They shared candy and tickled each other. She was happy to go north, the mother said.

The mother claimed she cried when her baby left but added that Maria didn't. In fact, she claimed that her daughter never even contacted her again. Although Maria later told the officers that her mother would call Pascual in America, demanding money from him and he'd send checks via mail to Guatemala.

While still living in Guatemala, Pascual tried to smuggle Maria to the United States on at least four different occasions. Each time they were stopped and sent back. Yet at no time did custom officers interview her. The fourth time he got lucky, and they made it into the United States and to Fort Myers, Florida. There they stayed with Matilde Pascual Andres, the trafficker's sister, in the middle-class neighborhood of Cape Coral. The sister had a common-law husband, Pascual Miguel Sebastian, who was making good money in the landscape business.

By that time Maria was fourteen and had already given birth to a stillborn child after Pascual punched her in the stomach several times to purposely rid her of the baby.

It didn't get any better for Maria. Once living in Cape Coral, Maria was awoken at four every morning and forced to clean, cook, do laundry and take care of Matilde's children. She couldn't leave the house for any reason. She was not allowed to attend school. She wasn't allowed to use the phone or talk to anyone at all. And she was raped and beaten on a regular basis.

Maria was left alone in the home while Pascual and his family went to the flea market or out to eat or out dancing. She was locked in her bedroom with a board over the window so she could not get out. Pascual told her if she attempted to leave he would call the police and the police would kill her.

Pascual gambled most of the time and when he lost, which was often, he would offer the girl to the men he owed money to in exchange for his debt. Many took him up on his offer and raped her. She lost count of how many times she was abused by different men. If she cried or complained, he would beat her and threaten her with a knife.

He even allowed his brother, Mario Pascual, to rape her in exchange for forgiveness on more debts and for their rent.

Soon she became pregnant again. When she was six months along, he came home and beat her for burning tortillas. She started bleeding and was in so much pain, Matilde panicked and rushed next door and asked the neighbor, Yoanna to help. She told Yoanna, "Maria's bleeding. She's complaining about stomach pains. Can you help us?"

Yoanna got Maria in car and took her to the emergency room of the local hospital. On the way to the hospital, Maria started pushing like she was in labor. When they arrived, she was rushed in for an emergency C-section. Maria's baby boy was born fifteen minutes later and weighed only one pound and three ounces. The newborn was taken immediately to the Newborn Intensive Care Unit.

Maria was given a room in the hospital. The social workers called the Cape Coral police department to report a possible domestic violence situation. Maria was only fifteen years old. Because she had been warned to never talk to the police, she didn't say very much. The police left without finding out very much. They didn't pay attention to the bruises she had received from Pascual or the fact that a fifteen-year-old girl had just had a C-section delivery. Pascual arrived a little while later and signed the birth certificate. Maria was released from the hospital, but the baby was kept there. Apparently since the police weren't going to anything, the hospital wasn't very concerned either.

Now Fernando's family would not allow Maria to go to the hospital to see the baby. The hospital staff was curious about the mother's absence but didn't have any contact information for Maria. They called Yoanna asking her what was going on. Yoanna brought Maria to her house where the hospital social worker could talk to her. Yoanna asked Maria if everything was okay. That was when Maria opened up and told Yoanna everything that had happened to her. Yoanna was quite upset and called the police demanding an investigation. A law enforcement officer came to interview Maria, but he claimed he could not understand the victim's language and suspended the case.

The concerned neighbor wouldn't let it rest and kept calling and calling, until finally, a Department of Children and Families Services investigator called again and, after more investigation, agreed that Maria was being mistreated. It was decided it would be best to take her out of the house. Unfortunately, until they could find anywhere more suitable, they placed Maria across the street at Yoanna's house.

Pascual came to Yoanna's house and threatened Maria. Yoanna eventually took her to the courthouse to file for a restraining order since the trafficker was harassing and threatening them. The restraining order was never served because the clerk lost the paperwork.

From there Maria was taken out of the foster home and placed in a shelter for unwed mothers. By the time we got the case Maria's son was almost three years old. Maria was a very smart girl with beautiful long hair. She attended school, was very happy, and maintained a spirit of her own. She loved American music and learned English very quickly.

Yet because of what she had been through along the way she developed a defense mechanism in order to survive. She was sweet but now liked to be the center of attention. One day they called me from the shelter asking me to talk to her regarding a behavioral issue. As we talked, she got up and threatened to slap me in the face before storming out of the room. Less than five minutes later she came back and told me, "I love you, please forgive me, Mom."

At seventeen, Maria started having issues at the shelter and started running away. Interestingly enough, she would always call the office early in the morning to tell me what she had done and allow me to pick her up and take her back. The next time she ran away, I decided to take her to the Children's Network.

Shockingly, she told me that she would rather be with her trafficker than at the shelter. When I pushed her for an explanation, she claimed she was being harassed by shelter staff. They were calling her stupid and ignorant and forcing her to clean and cook for the others.

I brought Maria to see the director of the Children's Network. She explained to him how she was being mistreated at the shelter. The director told me that Maria was going to be removed from the shelter and he was going to start an investigation. A couple of days later I received a phone call from the county. I was asked if I was providing any kind of financial help to the shelter. I said yes, I had been paying them $1,500 for each victim of human trafficking that they were caring for. An investigation found out that the shelter was triple-dipping—getting funding from me, the county and the state.

The system continued to fail Maria. She was being victimized by the ones that were supposed to help her. The shelter blamed FCAHT for having her removed, but I have no regrets. The shelter was more concerned with the numbers than the people they were supposed to be helping.

Maria and her child were placed in a foster home. When Maria turned eighteen, she was able to move into another program and establish an apartment with her son and is now doing well.

This case proved very demanding on my private life. From start to finish the entire case had been a series of missteps, blatant physical and sexual abuse disregarded by hospital staff, court inaction, lost petitions and law enforcement neglect. It was incredible state of affairs. From the start, the police had been notified about a possible sex abuse incident and it seemed they brushed it under the carpet. No arrests were made at the time because the police said there was no indication of any wrongdoing and no evidence of slavery and the girl was uncooperative. Uncooperative? More like scared of everyone around her.

The outcome of the case was swift when it finally came to justice. Three Guatemalans were arrested on federal human trafficking charges and accused of smuggling and enslaving Maria in southwest Florida. Fernando Pascual, then twenty-two, was sentenced to ten years in prison. Pascual's sister, Matilde, and his brother-in-law were also given prison sentences for their roles in harboring the young girl.

Maria is now safe in southwest Florida with her son. She's graduated from school and is attending college while her son is attending school. She is in a stable relationship and is doing great.

A year or so after Maria's case, I was asked to work with producers on a film about human trafficking called *Lives for Sale*. The documentary partially filmed in southwest Florida, included the case of Maria in Lee County.

It was strange seeing her story up on the big screen during the screening in New York but the movie helped significantly to raise awareness of modern-day slavery and the ignorance surrounding it.

I soon realized there was still so much training and education left to do. I hadn't scratched the surface yet. And it wasn't just in this country. I needed to join forces with other groups and reach out to those who needed me.

I still found it hard to understand how a parent could sell a child to someone for a handful of money. I tried to speak to parents who had sold their children for cash. One man told me that he had sold his daughter into a lifetime of prostitution for the benefit of the family, so the family could eat. He was quite pleased because she still sent money back. His next daughter in line was soon coming of age, and by the look in his eye, it wouldn't be long until she too suffered the same fate.

There are reports that these transactions are occurring a lot younger than people realize. Children as young as ten are now hopping the borders in search of jobs. Their parents, often encouraging them, are blind to the dangers they could face along the way, thinking only of the money they could see as a result.

You're My Angel

The fall of 2006 was another very busy year in the world of human trafficking. I was invited again to Washington, DC. This time to meet one of my heroes and favorite singers of all time—Ricky Martin. Ricky had become a major player in the fight against human trafficking, and he was speaking at a Congressional hearing on the subject.

I was almost as nervous as when I met President Bush. Ricky was, and still is, one of my daughter's idols. She used to have photographs of him plastered all over the walls of her bedroom when she was growing up. I had taken her to see him in concert about a year earlier. The concert was one of the best I've ever seen. Ricky was amazing.

On the day I was to meet Ricky, I waited in the hotel lobby, hands sweating, wondering if I was slightly overdressed. I remember it was about eleven o'clock in the morning. The Executive Director of Ricky's Foundation came to get me and escorted me to his suite. As I walked in to the main room, I saw a white grand piano by the window of his hotel suite. The huge suite was very bright and on one of the top floors. A few minutes later, Ricky appeared out of a side room dressed all in white with no shoes on his feet. My jaw hit the floor. He was much better looking in the flesh than on the TV, and to be honest, he's not bad looking on TV. He gave me a huge hug and a kiss on the cheek.

"Anna it's great to meet you. Thanks for coming," he motioned for me to sit down.

I felt light-headed and had to hold onto the chair to make sure I didn't fall over. He sat across from me, hugging a chair cushion while we talked and talked. He was such a lovely human being, very simple in his approach. He was not arrogant, just very spiritual. I felt so comfortable and so peaceful in his presence. We discussed human trafficking and some of the cases I had been involved in. I told him all about Chica and my other experiences.

He sat and listened, eyes open wide, asking question after question. He appeared so interested, taking in everything I said. When I finished, he smiled and simply added, "Anna, you really are my hero… thank you for doing what you're doing… you're personally making so much difference."

I had to keep a tight grip on the glass of water I was holding to keep from dropping it.

"I look up to you," he added, "You are so much an inspiration for all the things you have done."

The Director stared at me. "What do you think of this?" he handed me the speech he and Ricky had put together for the congressional hearings later that day. "Would you add or change anything?"

I read it, clarifying some questions regarding the human trafficking laws and told them I thought it was fine.

Ricky thanked me again. We just had a special connection. I felt as if I had known him for a long time.

At first I thought it was all just a publicity stunt, but the more I spoke with him the more I realized that he truly cared about the issue and the victims.

Ricky wanted his foundation to be prominent in times of natural disaster such as floods, hurricanes, tsunamis and earthquakes. He wanted to provide aid to the youngest survivors and their families.

He told me he wanted to join forces with other organizations around the world like mine to really start to make a difference. The more he talked, the more I realized everything Ricky and his team supported was exactly what I believed in as well.

I became a good friend and was thrilled when he asked me personally to be one of the mentors for his foundation. I didn't hesitate and soon after I became active with the Ricky Martin Foundation, providing him with a list of important people in DC and the country to help him with his *Llama y Vive*, Call and Live, campaign. This was a campaign in partnership with Banco Internacional de Desarollo and the International Organisation for Migration with the goal of raising awareness on human trafficking in Latin America and to promote national hotlines for prevention and support for the victims. It proved a huge success. As a result of these campaigns in places like Costa Rica, the Dominican Republic, Ecuador, Nicaragua and Peru, well over 33,000 phone calls have been received through the national hotlines. What 's more, these calls fostered over 170 police investigations, and approximately 6,000 potential victims of human trafficking have received life-saving information while helping to lock up many perpetrators and criminals.

Ricky has done a fine job. His efforts have been recognized within the world of human trafficking. He's received a Hispanic Heritage Award for his humanitarian work through the Sabera Foundation in rescuing three orphaned girls from the streets of Calcutta. He also acts as a Goodwill Ambassador to UNICEF, and established the Ricky Martin Foundation in Puerto Rico to advocate for the welfare of children around the world. His messages against human trafficking are always from his heart. I am so honored to call him my friend, my brother and my colleague.

Not long after meeting Ricky, about two weeks prior to Thanksgiving in 2006, I received a phone call from a shelter concerning a possible victim of sexual assault who had suddenly disappeared. They believed she had probably gone, or was sent, back to her homeland of Guatemala. All they could tell me was the girl, Eva, had been living with her foster parents when the wife reported finding her husband engaged in a sexual act with the girl. At the time Eva was just sixteen. She told the wife he raped her and it wasn't the first time. She said he had raped her for almost two years since she'd been in their care.

Not surprisingly, the police got involved, and the husband was arrested and dragged off to jail. Originally, he was charged with unlawful sexual activity and battery, both second-degree felonies punishable with many years in prison. However, after investigation the charges were changed to sexual battery by a person of familial or custodial authority. He now faced up to thirty years in prison if convicted.

In the meantime, Eva was moved to another foster home for her protection. The wife soon realized just how serious the offence was and how long the punishment would be for her husband. She started to back track on her story and laid all of the blame on Eva. She told the police she had made a mistake and that Eva was lying. She maintained her husband's innocence.

The wife started turning up at the girl's new home and harassing her. She called her names: a whore and a slut. She followed her around telling her that because of her lies, her husband would now die in prison.

After a while, the wife changed her approach. She dropped her aggressive style. She started pleading with Eva, explaining that her husband didn't mean to harm her. He liked her. They both did. She told her that if she stayed here and testified, he would go to prison for a long time.

She somehow persuaded Eva she should move away for a while.

Finally, the girl agreed to go back to Guatemala for a few months until everything blew over. The only problem was that Eva didn't have a passport. However the wife wasn't going to let such a small technicality ruin her plan.

One night without informing the authorities, or Eva's new foster parents, the wife drove Eva to Eva's sister who was staying in a teenage mother shelter. At the shelter, Eva took her sister's passport without her sister's knowledge.

Eva didn't look anything like her eighteen-year-old sister but that didn't matter. The woman bought the girl a one-way ticket and Eva was hurried through customs in Miami airport showing the wrong passport. No one noticed and she didn't get stopped, not even questioned as she rushed Eva through the ticket counter and TSA in the United States and immigration in Guatemala. And this was after September 11, 2001, when security was supposed to have been tightened.

With the witness now back in her homeland there would be no plaintiff, and with no plaintiff, there would be no court case.

It was the perfect crime, until the police and her social worker got suspicious and started to ask questions. They didn't believe Eva could have paid for or arranged an international flight. They assumed someone had helped her or pushed her to do it. The police instantly revoked the husband's bond for the possibility of tampering with a witness.

Out of the blue, I got a call from the authorities asking me if I could help them find Eva in Guatemala. I had a good relationship with the consulate office and the government of the country through my work, and they thought I would be their best hope. During an arranged meeting, I was told all about the case and the repercussions of Eva's absence from the case.

But I had to go find her. I felt like a soldier about to parachute behind enemy lines to find a prisoner of war.

I immediately started making phone calls to people who I thought could help. Rebecca Drucker is a good friend of Ricky Martin's and donated the airline tickets using her own mileage to cover the cost. She did this on behalf of Ricky Martin Foundation. She is an amazing person that I respect and admire for her good heart. I was also able to get some money from other organizations to assist with hotel, meals and transportation from Guatemala City to Aldea Tataj, where Eva lived.

With my travel arrangements sorted, I needed to find out some more information about the case and Eva herself. I arranged to meet with Eva's sister at the shelter. The girl broke down into floods of tears on seeing me. The wife had brought Eva to the shelter. She had Eva take her sister's passport without the sister's knowledge. Eva's sister didn't even notice that her passport was missing until many days after Eva had left.

She told me how they had been smuggled in from Guatemala to Florida by a relative. They came to the United States to work and sent the money they earned back to Guatemala. When they first arrived in Fort Lauderdale they stayed at their uncle's house. They both cleaned and cooked for everyone living at the house and Eva's sister, who was older, also worked as a housekeeper at a nearby hotel.

The sister became pregnant at the age of sixteen by one of the house occupants. The situation was reported to the Department of Children and Family Services by the hospital when she gave birth. Eva and her sister were taken away and placed in a foster home.

Later they were moved from Fort Lauderdale to Fort Myers where they were split up. Eva was placed with the foster family and her sister and her baby were placed at a shelter.

"Please get her back," her sister said to us, "I miss her so much."

"I will," I promised her.

With everything ready in Guatemala, I flew out of Miami airport accompanied by the director of the shelter who decided to come with me. During the flight I sat quietly near the window, contemplating what I would find when we got to Guatemala.

Not knowing what I would find scared me half to death. This was my third trip to Guatemala, but during my first two trips I never went further than Guatemala City. Guatemala is the size of the state of Tennessee, according to National Geographic Kids. It is bordered by Mexico in the north, Belize and the Caribbean on the east, Honduras and El Salvador to the south and the Pacific Ocean to the west.

We arrived at Guatemala and the first night we stayed at the Crown Plaza Hotel in Guatemala City. Early the next morning I made contact with Casa Alianza, an organization that supports street children in Guatemala. They mainly work with orphaned, abused or abandoned street children who have been traumatized by their situations.

They provided us with a social worker and a rather casual-looking driver to go in search of Eva. The social worker told us that hopefully the government of Guatemala would make arrangements to help us with the immigration documents to be able to fly back to the United States on our return.

Although Guatemala is a very beautiful country, it is also a place high up the list for human trafficking. It's not surprising when almost three quarters of the indigenous Mayan people live well under the poverty line. A typical family has at least six children. Survival is hard, so the offer of money for one of their children is not only tempting but they foolishly believe it will help their family and their child have a better life.

I was aware of stories of fathers hawking their daughters for money or livestock or old beaten up cars. Tales like this are common in these parts. Kids are sold daily; virgins go for a higher price. One person once told me her grandfather sold his aunt for a sheep. Twenty dollars means a family can survive for a few weeks; two hundred dollars is a fortune in this part of the world.

We took off on the long trek to Aldea Tataj in an old rusty red van with a stick shift which the driver crunched violently with every gear change. The trip was a long, scary drive. One I will never forget. As we headed out of the city, the roads were wide and reasonably well maintained, but once we got higher up into the mountains that all changed. They got narrower and more treacherous. In fact, I wouldn't even call them roads, more like small dirt tracks, covered in potholes, cut into the side of the high rambling mountains.

On occasions, there was only room for one car at a time to pass in either direction. Our red van inched dangerously along balancing on the edge on the cliff. Due to the moisture and the dirt, the van kept skidding sideways. Looking down at the canyon below with no sight of the bottom was terrifying.

Guatemala has thirty volcanoes and three of the volcanoes were still active. The smoke bellowing out of the mountaintops made our climb appear surreal. I prayed harder than I had ever prayed in my life.

Just when I thought our journey couldn't get any worse, a thick fog descended and stayed with us for the rest of the trip. It got so bad I could hardly see a few feet outside the window, which at the time was probably the best thing. I'm still not sure how the driver kept us on the road. It was very cold, and it was very humid.

I held my colleague's hand tightly and prayed we would make it. During the trip we stopped a few times for food or toilet breaks. But the bathroom stops were a nightmare due to the dirt and stink at many of the locations by the side of the road and often there was no toilet paper.

It took us almost fourteen hours to get to the remote village of Aldea Tataj. We arrived around midnight. It wasn't a big place, quite a small village with small houses and farms dotted around on the side of the mountain.

We were told by the social worker to be careful. In Guatemala, the villagers don't trust outsiders coming to the village to "take away" their children. She told us a story of how a Japanese tourist and his Guatemalan bus driver were beaten to death with sticks by the locals after the Japanese tourist took a photograph of a young girl. Across the country, foreigners were seen as devils or demons that appeared from nowhere to steal their children in the night.

Right on cue, our driver showed us a large wooden club he had under the seat. "Just in case," he said.

Thank God he never had to use it.

Even in the darkness, the houses looked poor. There were no side streets, just one main road running through the village.

Without knowing where Eva lived, we started knocking on doors of the small houses. Some people ignored us, closing the door in our faces, others didn't bother to answer. Then our first bit of luck. An elderly man pointed out a house with a green door at the end of the street. The fog was thicker and now the night air had turned icy cold. I knocked on the door, shivering, tired and hungry. We waited. It opened. It was her. Eva stood there, staring at us. She recognized my colleague immediately and grabbed a hold of her.

"What are you doing here? Come in… come in," she said excitedly.

The house was small and cramped, rustic with no furniture except for a wood bench. On the side they had a small bin with corn and very limited supplies. There were no beds, just pine needles on the floor covered by colorful homemade blankets. No TV, or phones, and no computers— things a teenager would have taken for granted in America. The bathroom was outside, and they had to get water from well in the back, which was very cold.

Eva had four siblings living with her. They were all much younger. We had some candy with us and gave them some. The little kids smiled and ate the candy as if they hadn't seen or tasted anything like it before. It broke my heart.

We spoke to Eva and her parents. Her mother looked very old for her age and was sick. I explained to them she was not in any kind of trouble.

Eva told me how the wife had ordered her to go back home or her husband would die in prison. She was a very shy and beautiful girl. She was so pleased to see us. Since she had been in the United States for over a year, her English was very good and I could see by the way she looked and the way she spoke that the American culture was already a big part of her life. She told me she found it very hard to come back to her village in Guatemala. She knew deep down that even though she had been abused by the husband, coming back here meant there would be no future for her. She had been really looking forward to graduating from high school and pursuing a higher education back in America. Coming back had depressed her and she didn't know what to do.

I talked to Eva again. Although she longed to go back to America, she was still too scared. I tried to convince her to come back with us and testify in court for what this man had done to her. I assured her that there was nothing to be afraid of. He was only her foster father and what he had done was not right.

I reasoned with Eva and told her that we did not want her foster father to do this to another child. I explained to her that by her coming back with me and testifying in court, she would stop the same thing happening to another child that might be placed in that same foster home. So then another child would not have to go through what she had to go through.

"Okay," she finally agreed, "I will come back with you."

I could tell her parents didn't want her to go, but they didn't stop her.

We got ready as quick as we could. The only downside was that now we had to get back in the old rusty red van and head back to the airport, now with another passenger.

We needed to get back so we didn't even stay the night. Outside it pelted down rain and the noise of the raindrops bounced off the sheet-metal roof.

Tired and exhausted, we headed off. I would like to say the journey back was better, but I would be lying. It was a mirror image of our previous expedition through the dangerous mountains in just as poor visibility. Unbelievably the fog seemed even thicker, the mountains steeper and the drop off even more treacherous looking.

I wasn't the only one praying for our safety. I have never felt so frightened in my life.

One on sharp bend our van nearly careened off the side of the road. The driver skidded, and the van stopped inches from the ledge. We all held our breath, afraid to breathe.

"Let's stop somewhere," I said to the driver when we continued, "This weather is too bad!"

Everyone agreed. We stopped in a small old town to get some sleep. It must have been around three thirty in the morning. The town was very small; the roads were very narrow. As we were driving I saw this white and blue building. The paint was old and peeling. There was a sign that said: "Beds for Rent." The room was again small and very cold. Cockroaches crawled through holes in the wall and scurried across the floor. We all slept with our clothes on, covered with three blankets each. The shower was lukewarm and sometimes freezing water would spurt out.

When I finally did manage to fall asleep, I didn't wake up until seven thirty in the morning. We still had a long way back to Guatemala City.

The first thing I did when we arrived at the Crown Plaza hotel was take a long, hot shower! It was the best feeling in the world.

Cleaned and refreshed, we sat in the room talking. Suddenly Eva started crying.

"What's wrong?" I asked, holding her young hand.

She sobbed uncontrollably.

"What's wrong Eva?" I repeated, "You will be okay… I promise nothing will happen to you."

"You saved me Anna, you and Mary." She stared at me tearfully.

"We didn't do anything!" She didn't let me finish.

"You don't understand," she whispered. "I was miserable and felt like taking my life. I had gone up the mountain, and I saw a tree. I found some rope. I was going to hang myself, commit suicide. I started praying and I asked God to send me an angel to help me and he sent you guys." Then she added, "My prayers were answered because you came to rescue me… you were the angels from God."

"What did you say?" I asked, shocked.

"You're my angel, Anna." Her words etched into my mind, embedded onto my brain. "You and Mary are my angels."

We all cried and hugged each other. I felt as though I was in a movie,

"Eva…Eva," I said, "Don't ever do that… nothing is worth that."

It was one of the sweetest, but saddest things I had ever heard.

I am thankful that sometimes I get signs that I'm on the right track. And as long as God gives me good health and keeps me going the way I'm going, I will continue.

The next day we started making arrangements to get Eva's travel documents in order to fly back to Florida. But Eva was a minor and we needed her parents to be present and sign the paperwork for the passport. We tried to persuade the authorities, explain the situation, but they wouldn't budge.

We made arrangements for her parents to take a bus to Huehuetenango, and we met with them and took them to a hotel. I remember Eva's parent's faces when they saw the room, especially the bathroom. I also remember when we took them for dinner at Pollo Campero and Eva's mother put the chicken and fries inside her bag so she could take it back home for the other kids.

Before we left, we gave Eva's mother money for groceries. We then went to the airport and Eva's father authorized her to fly back with us. The driver and social worker from Casa Alianza in Guatemala took her parents back to Huehuetenango so they could take the bus back to Aldea Tataj.

It was Thanksgiving Day, and we were able to catch the afternoon flight back to Miami and then the evening flight from Miami to Fort Myers.

We arrived back to Fort Myers at ten o'clock Thanksgiving night. Even though I missed Thanksgiving dinner with my family, it was probably the best Thanksgiving I have ever had. Just to be there to see Eva and her sister reunited was worth everything.

Eva overcame her fears and testified in court. The husband was found guilty and is still serving time in prison. Eva went back to school and graduated with honors. Eva and her sister are finally together. Her sister got engaged and attended college. She also was able to visit her family in Guatemala and took her son to meet his grandparents. I have lost contact with them, but I still pray for them every day.

Go Home or Else!

In early 2006 there was a dreadful news bulletins concerning a couple from Brazil, now living in Florida, whose baby had been stolen. The mother had been walking on the street with a friend and their babies. Someone offered them a ride. They decided to get in to the car and that is when the male driver dropped her friend off but kept the mother and baby in the car and sped off. Later the driver stopped the car, pushed the mother out and took off with the baby.

The grieving faces of the poor mother and father on the television screen trying to keep from having a complete melt down while being interviewed by reporters was heartbreaking.

"The parents didn't know who or why someone would do such a thing," the reporter concluded, "But police believe the baby boy may have been kidnapped."

As I was watching the news, I kept seeing some indicators that they were not truthful with law enforcement. An Immigration and Customs Enforcement agent called me on the phone and I advised her of my observation and she agreed with me. She filled me in about the couple and how the police had just found out they were illegally living in the United States after getting smuggled across the border several months before.

"Thing is," she talked to me in confidence, "They are so nice and seemed quite genuine, but we did a routine polygraph on both of them and the results were inconclusive."

"Oh," I said, knowing full well how accurate these types of tests were. "Do you suspect they're hiding something?"

She replied, "I don't know… but something isn't right. They are definitely holding something back as if they are afraid to tell us what."

I suggested she do a human trafficking assessment just in case and she agreed. A human trafficking assessment questionnaire lists questions aimed at helping professionals assess the possibility of a human trafficking case. It's not full proof but can be a good guide if used correctly. What I like about the assessment is that it also gives the interviewer many useful hints and tips to make the interviewee more relaxed for optimum accuracy.

The following day the ICE agent called me just to let me know the investigation was changing from kidnapping to human trafficking, That is when she explained to me that they did the assessment and they found out that they had a smuggling debt that was outstanding and apparently they had been threatened and feared the baby was taken in exchange for the debt. Then the ICE agent thanked me for my input.

Several months earlier the couple made their way up from Brazil and was given the name of a man who would get them across the border. They agreed to pay the coyote around $5,000 to smuggle the two of them and their newborn baby across the border into America.

The crossing wasn't easy and took them several days longer than expected due to tighter security at the border and the added complication of the newborn. Once in the United States, the coyote changed his mind about the price and almost doubled it from his original asking price to around $9,000.

The couple couldn't afford the increase, but not to upset the smuggler, they said they would get the money in the next few days. He told them in no uncertain terms that if he didn't get what was rightfully his, they would face the consequences. In a panic the couple went into hiding from the coyote. What they didn't appreciate was that it wasn't easy to just disappear. The trafficker had a tight web of informers he used to track them down.

One day a note appeared under the couple's door instructing them that either they pay their debt by the end of the week or something terrible would happen. Human smugglers have a ruthless reputation, often savage in the things they will do to get money they believe they are owed.

The couple failed to get the money together. Less than a week later, their baby went missing.

Before going to the police, the couple tried to contact the smuggler to tell him they were sorry and would do whatever they could to get the money to him and that they just wanted their child back.

Unfortunately, there was no happy ending to this couple's story. They never saw the smuggler or their baby ever again. The smugglers are callous, brutal and heartless.

I'm speculating that the baby was sold on the black market for a lot more than the few thousand dollars the couple owed. The going rate for healthy babies in Central and South America, I've been reliably informed, can be anywhere up to $30,000. Newborns are highly valued and with such a growing market, babies are being targeted more and more by traffickers.

I've heard stories of human traffickers turning up in hospitals and taking babies out of the nursery. In South America, a masked man approached a woman in broad daylight, held a knife up to her throat and threatened her, before taking her baby and disappearing into the street. Again the baby was never found.

They also target pregnant women, either kidnapping them or offering more false promises. They string the woman along until they can sell the newborn. Babies are put up for sale on the black market, where the profits usually are divided up between the traffickers, the doctors, and others involved in the illegal process. Sometimes the mother gets a small fee but in a lot of the cases, nothing at all.

This takes human trafficking and kidnapping to a completely different level. It made me realize I needed to work harder to fully get to grips with the business and the twisted minds that prosper from it.

I thought it would help if I visited other countries with different cultures to find out what kind of issues they were facing and to learn how they were dealing with human trafficking.

Luckily, the news of all the good work my team and I had been doing in America was quickly spreading far and wide. Due to this, I got an invitation to speak at their first human trafficking training conference in the city of Buenos Aires in Argentina in 2006, a major honor for me. I'd always been a fan of Eva Perón, the second wife of President Juan Perón, who served as the First Lady of Argentina from 1946 until her death in 1952. I'd read lots of books on her incredible life and of course saw the movie *Evita* several times.

When I arrived in the city, the reception I was given by the event organizers and the people of the country was first rate. As soon as I landed, they couldn't do enough for me. However it wasn't just their hospitality that impressed me, it was also how knowledgeable about the subject of human trafficking most of the people were. They knew about the work

I had been involved with and asked lots of questions. Later that night I went for a meal with the organizer and some of the other delegates. We talked all night about how Argentina was equipping itself to face up to the growing battle against modern-day slavery.

What I didn't realize until that time was how entrenched human trafficking was within the country. It is difficult to estimate just how big the problem was because Argentina is not only a country of source, but it also transports many victims into the major cities from other places like Paraguay and Brazil.

The government was trying hard to understand and improve the situation by introducing anti-trafficking laws. They set out a campaign, *No to Human Trafficking, No to Modern-day Slavery,* with the aim to bringing to the Argentinean public's attention how much of an issue this criminal activity was. Progress was slow and it's still proving hard work with very few convictions compared to the number of human trafficking victims identified.

According to the non-government organization Casa del Encuentro, during an eighteen-month period more than six hundred women were reported to have been abducted from the rural areas. However many believe that for every one of those there were at least six others taken into slavery but never reported. They were and still remain invisible. And just like many other countries, there are reports of large-scale corruption amongst many of the police officers and government officials which ensure a blind eye is turned to what's going on. False documents can be easily obtained and there are numerous examples of brothels being tipped off before raids take place. The network of organized crime that connects the vast countryside to the big cities is like the roots of an oak tree.

Human trafficking was evident to me just by scanning advertisements appearing in the local newspapers. Several stated they were on the lookout for country girls with no experience but who wanted to travel to the capital where they would be guaranteed to earn good wages in well-run companies. With more than forty percent of the population living in poverty, the advertisements must be tempting to poor, unemployed girls looking for a better future for themselves and their family. Reality was much different. Police in the northwestern province of Jujuy received more than fifty reports of missing young women in a three-month period.

All of them had gone to see about an exciting job that they had read in the local newspaper and were never heard from again.

On the pages of the same newspaper, more sinister advertisements targeted men looking to meet "daring university students", or "erotic little dolls", or a "new bunny fresh from the countryside" or "just in from the south", a clear link between the two sets of advertisements.

Besides these suspect job advertisements, blatant kidnapping is also a common method used. Many women have been taken from their villages to the cities or across the border to other countries. Whichever their fate, the girls, like many in the United States, are left without money and documents, probably locked up, isolated, beaten and raped. The same old routine with the same old methods but being played out in a different country.

After I came back from the meal with the organizers that first night I sat in my hotel room checking my email and quickly going through the presentation I had put together about human trafficking and victim services.

I phoned my husband and children to tell them I'd missed them so much and I couldn't wait to get back home. We had planned a vacation and none of us could wait to spend some quality time together.

I put my computer away and sauntered towards the bathroom to brush my teeth before bed.

"What's that?" I thought to myself as I noticed a manila envelope pushed under my front door.

Probably the agenda, I thought, as I picked it up off the carpet and opened it.

Walking towards the bathroom, I stopped dead in my tracks, placing my hand up to my mouth in utter astonishment. I read it again, this time hearing myself reading the short note out loud.

"*Anna,*" it stated in scribbled red letters on the single piece of paper, "*pack up and go back to the airport now. Argentina's got no human trafficking here... go home or else.*"

Without thinking, I opened the door and looked up and down the long corridor of the four star hotel. There was no one there. I closed the door quickly and may sure it was bolted. I sat down on the edge of the bed, shaking. It brought back painful memories of the day I received the threatening phone call a few years prior. On that occasion, the call had scared me half to death, but to be truthful, now I was in a strange city in a strange country without my family around. I feared for my life. I didn't want to die; I was only trying to help.

Too stunned to cry, I picked the phone up. I wanted to talk to my husband. I started to dial but placed the receiver back down. I didn't need to worry him and the rest of my family. What could they do other than tell me to come home? This was the world I had decided to live in. This was my fight. Instead, I called one of the organizers staying in the hotel. Minutes later, several police officers knocked on my door. Later that night, two security guards were posted outside my door. Strangely, that night I slept very well. The next morning, I couldn't go anywhere without security following me. It was rather bizarre eating breakfast with two burly police officers watching me from the next table.

At the conference, more of the organizers came up to me to apologize. News had spread fast. Outwardly, I smiled bravely and told everyone I was all right and there was nothing to worry about. Inwardly I hoped I would be!

Needless to say, I was nervous about doing my presentation, even more than normal. As I sat there all kinds of terrible scenarios of what could happen to me whirled around in my head. I tried to push then to the back of my mind and stay focused.

When it was my turn to speak, all the nerves, the threats, all the fears disappeared as my passion for the subject drove me. When I finished, I received a standing ovation. The rest of my time there went without any more little surprises slipped underneath my door.

It turned out that the letter was written by an Argentine father whose daughter had been killed by traffickers. He thought I was brining harm instead of good. He was in the audience at my speech and apologized to me. We are in contact still today.

Thankfully I got invited back to the wonderful country many times. Since 2006 I have been helping Argentina with their human trafficking laws and to date I have provided nine other trainings sessions there. I feel very safe in Argentina and I have never had a threat on my life there since.

During the last few visits, I've been fortunate to meet the parents of girls who have gone missing. It's been so emotional. I meet them at the event and they all have pictures of their missing daughters on their shirts.

I also met another very special person and now a dear friend, Susana Trimarco. Trimarco has been fighting trafficking since her daughter, Marita Verón, disappeared in San Miguel de Tucumán, the capital of the Argentine province of the same name.

Marita was believed to have been kidnapped on a city street while walking to visit her gynecologist. She was twenty-three and had a three-year-old daughter. Apparently, a while later she was spotted working in two brothels in the province of La Rioja, but though her mother still holds out hope, so far she has never been located.

What *hasn't* helped Trimarco's search to find her daughter has been a wall of silence put up in front of her. Unbelievably, she has been given many false clues on her daughter's whereabouts, some genuine mistakes, many not. She has also been the target of death threats since she started on her quest.

Trimarco has dedicated her life to fighting the trafficking of women nationwide. She hasn't found her beloved Marita, but she has rescued hundreds of women who have been forced to sell their bodies in illegal brothels.

"In the search for my daughter, I've found numerous victims. I took them home and did as much as I could to help them. Soon, I realized I needed to do something bigger because I couldn't cope with the thought of losing my daughter on my own. With the support of Tucumán province's Secretariat of Human Rights, I created the María de los Ángeles Foundation. The María de los Ángeles Foundation provides aid to the victims and has helped educate judges, prosecutors and police officers deal with women trafficking," Trimarco said.

Marita Verón's story has become symbolic of the trafficking of women that plagues Argentina. Her disappearance has inspired many in Argentina including one of the most popular soap opera *Vidas Robadas*, or *Stolen Lives* in English, which premiered in March 2007 on Telefe.

Trimarco is an incredible determined, yet unassuming, woman. She really is my hero, and I don't say that lightly. I wish the world had a hundred more Susan Trimarcos. It would make my job a lot easier and a lot more rewarding.

At that first event in Argentina I met with many of the representatives from the Organization of the American States and since then I have been invited to be part of their training delegation. I have been working with them to deliver training on human trafficking ever since. It has taken me to all sorts of places—countries including Russia, Costa Rica, Mexico, Belize, Nicaragua, Guatemala, Panama, El Salvador, Chile, Peru, Uruguay, Ecuador, Suriname, Guyana, Trinidad & Tobago, Barbados, St. Lucia, St. Vincent, Grenada, Dominica, Antigua, St. Kitts, Jamaica, The Bahamas, Dominican Republic , Puerto Rico and of course Argentina—spreading the word. I have also been invited to speak by the other governments as a result of referrals from individuals who have attended my presentations and recommended me for other events.

The downside of all this was, of course, every week or so I was jumping on a plane to go speak at one of the many conferences springing up. My family saw less and less of me.

I've never been afraid to fly. When I was growing up in Puerto Rico my dad worked for Caribair, so we were able to get cheap flights and were always flying to various destinations on vacation. Even when we moved to Florida when I was in my teens, he worked for Eastern Airlines so stepping on and off planes was second nature to me, my sister and my stepbrother and stepsister.

But one flight to St. Thomas in particular will live with me forever. I was scheduled to fly on a full 757 from Miami to St. Thomas, Virgin Islands.

Everything started off fine until the pilot announced that due to bad weather in St. Thomas we could not land and we were going touch down in San Juan, a short twenty minute flight from the island, and probably spend the night there.

"Hopefully," he added, "The weather will be on our side and we will get away first thing in the morning."

After a sleepless night in a hotel with the air conditioning not working properly, I got to the airport the next morning only to be told the flight had be delayed yet again due to more bad weather. The issue was a subtropical depression named Otto that was situated north of San Juan and St. Thomas. The captain informed us that we couldn't take off yet because of extreme winds over St. Thomas but not to worry—as soon as a window of opportunity came, we would be off.

I kept communicating with the conference organizers in St. Thomas since I was supposed to be speaking later that afternoon. The wait seemed to go on for ages. Around one in the afternoon, we boarded the flight, but as we were taxiing down the runway, the plane stopped at the holding site.

"Sorry we will have to turn back around," the captain announced again.

I couldn't believe it. The pilot explained we had a problem with a computer malfunction and it needed to be checked out. It took us about forty-five minutes to have it fixed and then we finally took off from San Juan.

"At last," I muttered to the man sitting next to me.

Ten minutes into the flight, I wished we hadn't taken off. Our plane started shaking and bobbing going up and down. It felt like a ship on the ocean rather than a plane in the air. The supposedly short twenty-minute flight turned into a two-hour nightmare. We tried landing four times and the pilot had to abort the landing each time at the last minute. People were screaming, while others were praying. I remember praying and asking God to please protect us all.

The last attempt to land, the pilot went in hard and I was positive we were going to crash. I have never felt so close to death in my life as I did that day.

"We are going back to San Juan." The pilot, thankfully, decided to quit. "It is not safe and I do not want to risk our lives."

Just when I thought we were safe, he had to abort the landing in San Juan because of similar problems. After several more attempts at a different runway on a different island, we finally landed to one of the biggest cheers I'd ever heard from a plane full of terrified passengers. I had tears of joy running down my face. I closed my eyes and I said a long prayer to God thanking him for allowing me and everyone else to live. The flight to St. Thomas was eventually cancelled. So I never made the conference. I felt bad for letting them down but they understood because St. Thomas was on State of Emergency due to the bad weather. In fact, being too shaken to fly straight back to Miami, I stayed in San Juan an extra day to calm my nerves.

Although I've had my life threatened and nearly died in an airplane, the opportunity I had been given to travel helped me to understand how the trends of trafficking were changing. It has given me a better understanding of the problem and other types of trafficking that no one seems to talk about in the United States. It has shown me how child labor trafficking is on the rise and how new trends are springing up. I saw children as young as four selling candy or carrying wood on the streets of Guatemala, while others sold souvenirs to tourists in the Dominica. I learned how prostitution was legal in Panama and the trafficking law only protects female adults for sex trafficking only.

It helped me understand why we have human trafficking law in the United States. I have been able to learn more about the UN mandate and the different protocols that were ratified by the countries, including the United States. And it has given me an experience that not many agencies have in the United States

One of the tools I have readily used in my fight against trafficking is the sites the perpetrators of the crimes use themselves to find out where to find action when they visit new countries or cities.

The Internet has become the best method for traffickers to promote their business and their "merchandise". Craigslist and Backpage are only two of many sites available for clients to search. There are many others but I prefer not to contribute to their bank accounts.

The sites are sickening, beyond words. They pass information to each other and actually rate places they have been to and the young children they have been with like someone would rate a hotel or a new book they have just finished!

The Web sites are basically chat rooms between pimps/traffickers and clients. They provide information regarding the girls, prices, locations, hotels that allow guests to bring prostitutes to their room, rating of the girls and key words for the potential clients to use when soliciting. It also gives instructions on what to ask taxi drivers since many have connections with the pimps and work on commission. For example, "Sunday Punch" will get one connected with a prostitute. "Chocolate" will get one a condom. "Palito" will get them sex. "Happy ending" is a massage that ends in sex. "Fresh meat," a new girl. Prices are referred to as "donations" or "roses."

I have used the sites to my advantage. They are very helpful because every time I travel to different places, they help me understand what is happening in each and every country. Sex tourism is increasing all over the world. Part of my training is teaching law enforcement and prosecutors how and what to look for so they are able to find cases and most important identify and rescue potential victims.

In Guatemala I came up to a "live auction site" and immediately provided the information to law enforcement attending the training and they started an investigation right away. The girl on the block was eleven years old and the auction was active at $7,500 US dollars.

I have spent hours searching the computer to find these sites. It is sad to see that in many countries, the law enforcement doesn't have a Cyber unit and are not aware of such Web sites. So my aim during many of my training sessions is to highlight these sites and how to use them. Unfortunately, at one training event in the Bahamas, everything on my hard drive was suddenly wiped off due to a virus from connecting to a rogue site.

On one of my trips to El Salvador, I arrived at the airport and asked my driver if they had a problem with human trafficking in their country.

He shook his head violently. "No… no… not here… other places yes, but not here."

"Oh good," I replied. I didn't want to burst his bubble.

When I got to the hotel I had a quick shower then went across the street for something to eat. It was a beautiful night, comfortably warm as I sat looking out at the beautiful view across the bay. I sat alone, sampling the local cuisine and people watching.

After a while, I watched a girl approaching the restaurant carrying an armful of red roses. I guessed she must have been around nine or ten years old. She wore a native dress, a scarf wrapped around her head; one of her shoes had a hole in the toe. It was already ten thirty at night, quite late for a minor of that age to be wandering alone around any city. She walked around the tables, targeting the couples sitting there, hoping to make a sale. She was having no luck.

She came towards me.

"How much?" I asked.

Her eyes lit up, a wide smile on her pretty face.

"Sit down please," I asked her, pulling out a chair for her. She looked around nervously. One of the waiters came over to shoo her out. "It's OK… She's with me."

The girl sat down beside me. I offered her some bread rolls. She ate one and put the other in her bag.

"What's your name?" I asked.

"Nitchel. I'm nearly twelve," she replied with pride.

"It's late to be selling flowers. Why don't you go home and try and sell the rest tomorrow?" I asked.

"I can't go home until I sell them all," she replied. "My step-father is nasty… he will beat me if I do."

"Does he beat you often?"

She nodded her head.

"Where's your mother?"

"He beats her too."

I wanted to take her home with me.

"Do you want some cake?" I asked.

Again she nodded. I bought her a large piece of chocolate cake and all the roses off her, nineteen red roses.

She skipped away, waving and smiling at me.

The next morning I took the roses with me when I did my presentation. When I finished, I asked the audience the same question I'd asked the taxi driver the night before.

"Have you got a problem with human trafficking in your country, your city?"

The majority shook their head no. I held up the roses and told them about my encounter with Nitchel, the little girl I'd met the night before, the victim forced to sell roses or get beaten. "Isn't that human trafficking?" I asked.

At a training in the Caribbean I asked: "And what about this place?" I projected onto the screen a picture of a club located in the city center. "Did you know," I added, "if you go there and ask for a 'Sunday Punch' you will be brought a prostitute, many of which are most likely being forced to solicit against their will.

A low murmur rung out around the room.

"No… no," someone shouted out.

I showed them some of the advertisements and comments I had taken off the Internet about that certain club plus a few others.

"I'm from Florida… and have never been to your country before, but I probably know more about the sex trafficking and labor exploitation of children in this country than you do."

I could tell some were embarrassed, others still not believing me. "Okay," I said. "Let's go there."

Thirty minutes later a group of us left in two cars to the club. The assistant special counsel for the country was there with his wife and sat next to me. As the waiter came, I asked for a Sunday Punch and he gave me a smile and said he could not get me a Sunday Punch. I kept saying that a friend of mine came to visit and ordered a Sunday Punch and said it was very good. He again smiled and said ""Yes, it is very good but not for a female." The counsel was shocked.

We ordered food and drinks and watched as two guys and two girls walked in. The girls looked unhappy, and never made eye contact with anyone. One of the guys kept going to the bar looking for potential customers. Several times he brought a client to where the girls were. They talked for a while and we could see money being passed between the men. One of the girls took the client by the hand and led him outside. Fifteen minutes later she came back in alone. During the five hours there, the girls went outside six times with six different men. Also during all that time, the two pimps drank beer after beer while the girls were given nothing ... not even water.

The counsel was so shocked that as a result of the visit to the club and the training, the country is now looking to follow in the footsteps of St. Lucia with respect to human trafficking law initiatives.

Blood on Their Hands

By the summer of 2007, work was still a rewarding but emotional rollercoaster. I was concerned about funding the business as well as the pain and hardship that I witnessed day after day. It was really taking its toll on me. I was away for long periods of time and missed my children and husband, and they missed me.

But it wasn't just the welfare of my family and the stress of the job weighing me down. As more people wanted to enter the human trafficking fight, for reasons of greed rather than helping, I got discouraged. I built and lost a partnership with a woman interested in personal gain. I was drained.

But a case came along to re-energize me.

It was the day before Thanksgiving 2007 when I received a phone call from a detective working for the Human Trafficking Unit of the Lee County Sheriff's Office, advising me they were going to be interviewing a sixteen-year-old child from Honduras whom they believed was a potential human trafficking victim.

I had so much to do to prepare for Thanksgiving dinner and I had promised my husband after Eva's case that I wouldn't miss or be late for another family holiday. But I also knew that I couldn't turn my back on a potential victim, and the officer who called me on the phone sounded quite distressed. As soon as I put the phone down, my husband knew, with just one look at my face, there was no way to persuade me to forget about the call until the holiday was over.

"Okay," he shrugged, "don't be long… and be careful," he said in defeat.

The station was about an hour from my home. I arrived and was immediately escorted to a small room with a TV positioned on top of a wooden desk. The atmosphere in the room was tense, extremely gloomy. There was no interaction between anyone except for a quick couple of handshakes and a few mumbled words. I sat down in front of the TV set with two detectives and an FBI agent.

The image on the screen showed the interrogation room next to us. Inside, a boy with jet-black hair and suntanned skin sat on a chair, his elbows leaning on a table in the center of the room. Several clean white napkins, still there from the lunch the law enforcement officers had just finished lay on the table in front of him. Opposite him, a female detective, a writing pad in front of her, sat ready to interview him. The rest of the room stood sparse and white.

Dan was a tall but lean, good looking teenager. He was clean, wearing jeans and nice shirt. At the same time he appeared quite manic, wild in his actions, like an animal. His hands shook, his head darted nervously from side to side. He kept glancing behind him at the door as if he was afraid someone was behind him.

The detective asked him the usual opening questions—What is your name? Where are you from? When he started talking, I could hardly hear him—his voice so was quiet and he mumbled. He was very respectful and a bit shy. He explained how he set out on his journey from his small village in Honduras through Mexico into the United States to find a job. He smiled for a brief second. "I wanted to earn enough money to send some back to my mother. We are very poor. My village is very poor. I want to do my best to help."

During his long and often treacherous journey through the rugged terrain of Mexico, he came across three men in a mountain village one night. They started talking, and the men told him they were also heading to America and that he could join them if he wanted. They had two other teenagers travelling with them, a boy about thirteen and a girl about fifteen. Thinking it would be better and safer to travel in a larger group, he agreed with no idea anything was wrong.

At first, everything appeared above board, but pretty soon, the journey turned nasty. The men set upon the boy one night, kicking and punching him to the ground. They took all his belongings and his documentation. They placed a gun to his head and told him he was going to die. One man pulled the trigger; the gun barrel clicked but didn't go off. They dragged him to his feet and told him he was coming with them and that he now belonged to them. He had no idea what their intentions were.

From that moment on, Dan was scared but powerless to do anything about the situation. For the rest of the journey, he and the other kids were tied up at night and gagged. They were beaten if they couldn't keep up or if they fell. Sometimes the men beat them for nothing at all.

"They would take the girl into the bushes at night," he muttered. "I knew what they were doing to her. I could hear her screaming. I couldn't help her. I wanted to but couldn't. I was too scared."

The boy slumped down further and further in his chair. He stopped looking directly at the detective and started talking as if he was talking to himself. "We travelled day and night, over the mountains and through the wild forests. One night, the other boy and I were attacked by wild monkeys, six or seven of them," he said. "I don't know why they attacked—maybe the men had upset them."

He drank some water from a glass.

"The young boy was bitten badly, his legs and arms cut to shreds. He lay on the floor screaming, blood everywhere. I was lucky; they didn't bite me."

"What happened?" the detective asked.

"They found it funny, the men, making fun of the boy. But he was bad. He couldn't walk. He was in so much pain, and he had a fever. He was shaking all over."

The mood of his captors soon changed when they realized just how serious his injuries were. "The men tried to get him to walk. They beat him. Then they made me and the girl try to help him, but it was no good." Dan went quiet; he started sobbing. "They, no… we… we just left him… left him in the forest to die. They took his shoes and everything else he had on him… and we left I could hear him yelling for us to come back."

There was silence in both rooms. The boy placed his head on the table and covered both ears with his hands as if he was trying to block out the sound of the boy screaming. The detective made an excuse and left the room, obviously upset.

She came and sat with us as we discussed the horrific story Dan had shared. None of us was prepared for what he was about to tell us.

It took twenty minutes for him to regain his composure. He sat upright.

"Sorry," he apologized, "I didn't mean to get upset."

"It's okay," the detective replied. 'Please continue."

The detective asked him how he got into the country. He couldn't actually recall much about getting across the border. All he remembered was one day arriving at a house somewhere in Arizona. The house was quite large but dark, the curtains drawn most of the time. It smelled of sweat and tobacco.

"They stripped me to my underwear and tied me to a chair," he explained. "There were others, boys and girls, tied the same way. Eight of us all together. Sometimes more. All tied up in the same room."

He estimated they ranged in age from twelve to seventeen. They weren't fed, just getting water now and again. There were six Mexican men in the house at various times.

"On my first day," he muttered, "three of the men untied one of the girls. She was Hispanic, and she had black hair. I think she was from Central America.. They raped her in front of us… right there on the floor… each of them in turn… one by one."

I suddenly felt cold; goose-pimps crawled up my arms.

He continued. "They did it in front of us. I didn't want to watch, but they made me. She was screaming, bleeding. One man punched her hard on the side of her head. She slumped backwards. They carried on."

Tears ran down my face. One of the detectives next to me, a man who had been in the force for many years, put his head in his hands. I wanted the boy to stop talking. I didn't want to hear anymore.

"Did they do anything to you?" the detective asked.

"Yes," he seemed embarrassed, "They raped me, too… many times."

The detective began to ask something else, but the boy interrupted her. "They killed her." He took another mouthful of water.

"Who?" the female detective looked at him. "The girl?"

He shook his head. "No. Not that girl. One of the others. She was maybe fifteen, young, Mexican. They were raping her. She fought back. She bit one of them on the hand. He slapped her, and then punched her so hard he knocked her out. Then. Then…." he couldn't get the words out. "Then… he lay on top of her, his knees on her shoulders on the ground and then he cut her head off with a knife."

"What?" the detective almost yelled.

"He cut her head off, in front of us. And then he held it up, swinging it in our faces. And told us it was a warning to us all."

The detective next to me stood up. He kicked his chair over in anger.

"I could smell her blood," the boy added. "They left her body on the floor next to us for a few days to remind us of what would happen if we did something wrong. The men were laughing, joking about it. They were messing with her head."

The boy suddenly started shaking. He jumped up, grabbed the napkins off the top of the table, and began to clean his arms and hands with them frantically. "Her blood is on my hands. I could have helped her, protected her. I should have done more."

I couldn't believe he felt guilty, as if it were his fault. I sat there, tears flooding my face; it was one of the most appalling things I had ever heard. The female detective stopped the interview and left the room. She again walked to our room, her face ashen, she was crying. "I can't continue with this," she broke down.

I walked over to her, putting my arm around her for support. "You're doing fine." I tried to calm her down. "You have to go back. He's comfortable with you."

"I don't think I can," she said again.

"You must."

After a while she decided to go back in and to carry on with the interview. She was so strong. I don't think I could have done it. It was one of the most powerful interviews I have ever seen.

Dan explained the "softening period" where he was continually beaten, raped and threatened. He said after a while, the beatings and the rapes became less frequent except for new victims introduced to the house.

"How did you get away?"

"One night I tried to escape. The door was open and I ran, but they caught me." He paused, "They brought me back. Four of them, they beat me and then one of them did this to me in front of the others." He rolled up the left leg of his shorts.

A jagged eight-inch scar ran down the inside of his thigh. "They cut me with a knife, cut me and left me. They wouldn't let me go to the hospital."

Again he started to nervously clean his hands with the napkins.

"What happened?"

He slumped down. "I tried again. But, again, they were waiting for me. They brought me back."

He was beaten again and told if they caught him again they would kill him.

A few weeks later he said he jumped the fence one night and ran as fast as he could. "I met a lady that took me in and fed me and got me a bus ticket to Fort Myers so I could get away and stay with one of her relatives."

He arrived in Fort Myers and stayed with a man and woman. They were nice to him. At first.

"I worked doing jobs around the house for a while. Then they made me go with others to do painting jobs for a local company."

He never got paid. They would take all his money and threaten him if he complained. Although where he found himself was nothing compared to what he had been through in Arizona, it was still human trafficking, still slavery.

"They didn't beat me or do anything else to me, but I couldn't come and go and they never paid me."

During one painting job, he got friendly with a co-worker whom he trusted. Dan told him what was happening. The worker couldn't believe it and told him not to go back and that he could stay with him. The man was very nice and helped him get fake papers and found him a job at a restaurant. While working at the restaurant downtown, Dan accidently touched a live wire, got a massive electrical shock and fainted. He was rushed to the hospital and that is when Lee County Sheriff's Office human trafficking unit was called.

When the interview was over, the room was silent. We were all in shock, speechless. We felt anger for what he had to go through. We gathered up our things and left.

Because Dan was a minor, he was referred to the unaccompanied minor program, and they took over his case. Thankfully Dan had taken the first steps to a new normal life and although he will never, ever get over what he's been through, hopefully he has the rest of his life to see the good in the world and not just the bad. Later I found out he went back home to his mother.

I remember that afternoon going back to the car and crying. Being a Christian, I believe we are all God's creatures, regardless of skin color or accent, and I find it hard to understand how people can do these most evil things to anyone else. How can people treat other human beings like this? What kinds of monsters are out there taking advantage of vulnerable children who are just trying to work and help their families?

Back home I had another sad Thanksgiving Day. I sat across the table and looked at my children, hoping and praying they would never find themselves in a situation anything like what that poor boy and others have found themselves. I didn't eat much that day, just picked at my food.

Less than a week after hearing Dan's story, one of the most horrific and life-changing interviews I'd ever done, my services were needed again. This time I got a call from the hospital at Fort Myers regarding a girl from Guatemala who had appeared at a local hospital with a four-month-old baby who had been born with serious birth defects. He was blind and deaf and his brain was not fully developed. The mother, Mita, became irate and kept telling the staff that she wasn't a bad mother. That she had been held against her will on the edge of town and made to work in a terrible factory that caused her baby to get ill.

As I arrived to the hospital, the social worker took me to a room where they explained to me that the baby's chances at survival were slim.

I met with the Mita. She had scabs around the edges of her mouth. Her skin was dry. She had dark circles under her young eyes. She was twenty-two, and she didn't know how to read or write.

"I was smuggled from Guatemala to Texas, I think," she explained to me. "But I was sold at the border to a man because I couldn't afford to pay the smuggler the fee he was asking for." Her new trafficker took her to a rundown house with two other girls. There she slept on a stained and smelly mattress in a room with six other teenagers. The house had no furniture, and only one toilet.

Every night, she would be taken with the others in a van to a big chicken factory where they were made to clean the dead chickens and put them inside a liquid to clean them of bacteria. They were not given protective gloves or hand cream.

"Did you ever complain?" I asked, looking at the red marks on her hands.

"Yes," she nodded her head. "I told the supervisor my hands were itching and I had a rash all the way up my arms. He dragged me out of the line and slapped me hard across my cheek, and then he marched me back to my work area and told me to work twice as hard or else!"

"What did he mean 'or else'?"

She shrugged her shoulders. "I didn't want to find out," she replied.

Conditions in the factory were deplorable. It stunk of rotten meat; animal blood and chicken innards covered the floors. She had no proper personal protective work attire. They worked non-stop in a building with no windows and no natural light from nine at night until five in the morning for no pay. Supervisors monitored them constantly, threatening them or slapping them if they felt the victims were not pulling their weight.

"I stood all night, no breaks, no rest… I was so tired and felt so ill by the time it was over. I left there every night covered in mess."

Back at the house, Mita and the others had no real facilities to wash or bathe. No hot water, no clean towels. Food was scarce, with only one small meal a day given to them. Then they were ordered to go to bed. The traffickers locked all the bedroom doors and windows. Sometimes they would line up the occupants and make an example of one of them. It was brutal. Once Mita was punched and kicked and threatened with immigration if she tried to escape. Another time she was told by her captures she would be taken back to the border, beaten and left there to die.

"We were always sick, coughing, covered in rashes. We always had colds, she explained.

At the house Mita got friendly with another victim, a boy about the same age as she. She got pregnant, and they decided to run away together. They headed to Florida where the baby was born.

The doctors at the hospital felt the baby's disability and medical condition could have been a result of the chemicals used to clean the chickens or any of the other appalling conditions she came in contact with at the factory.

I took Mita and her child to a shelter and made sure she had all the medications they both needed. While we were having dinner, I noticed her stomach was swollen. I hoped it wasn't what I suspected but took her to the doctor and found out she was pregnant again.

Not the best timing or circumstance.

This time however, we made sure she had good prenatal care. Six months later, she delivered a healthy baby boy.

Although the initial prognosis for her first child was dire, he lived. We were able to get him enrolled in programs to help her deal with his special needs. I also spoke with the local priest and had both kids baptized at her request.

The doctor who delivered her second baby recommended she be put on birth control due to the high risk of having another baby with some type of birth defect. Mita agreed. I had no say in her decision. The case manager was there to support her. She did not chastise her or try to force her own religious beliefs on Mita. We need to respect the victim's decision whether they share our beliefs or not. We are here to guide and empower these victims, not control them as their traffickers had. We must give them back their right to choose.

The coalition had been receiving funding from a Catholic organization. They were disappointed, even with the doctor's recommendation, that we supported Mita's choice to use birth control. The organization canceled our contract.

Mita's case was investigated by a federal agency but was closed because they could not find the location of the house or the chicken factory since she could not provide them with any addresses. ICE refused to certify her because she could not provide an address even though she had complied with all their mandates.

I feel like we failed her. We had to transfer her to another agency because the care she required exceeded our funding. We connected her with an immigration attorney and paid for three months of her apartment rent.

Boca '39

After my rescue missions to countries like Guatemala and my training events in Argentina, it wasn't long before I was off on my travels once more. This time I crossed the Atlantic Ocean to attend the UNDOC Human Trafficking conference in Vienna, Austria, in 2008. The UNDOC is the United Nations Office on Drugs and Crime.

I'd never been to Europe before, and I was really looking forward to it. Because of the expense of the trip and my kids going to school, my husband, yet again, volunteered to stay home alone and play house dad.

Unfortunately, during the journey I became a victim myself. Not of human trafficking, but of another fast growing crime, identity theft. Someone stole my debit card details when I was traveling through one of the airports during the connections, and before I realized, they had emptied out my bank account.

When I arrived in Vienna, I had a massive panic attack in the lobby of my hotel when my card was declined. I checked the account myself and found no money in there at all. Devastated and almost inconsolable, I didn't know what I was going to do. I had only brought enough cash for a taxi and a meal. The hotel staff was wonderful and completely understanding.

I contacted my husband. It was still the middle of the night in Florida, but he told me immediately not to worry. Within a few hours he'd sent me money via Western Union so I could survive for the week. I still felt terrible and I wanted to go home but my husband convinced me to stay and assured me everything would be just fine.

To cheer myself up I went for a stroll around the city. It was beautiful. Much better than I'd ever dreamed it would be, with its rich, gothic-style architecture, unlike anything I'd ever seen in the United States. I wandered around the streets all morning in complete awe.

Pretty soon I forgot about my troubles and headed off to the conference. When I got there, I was amazed that so many people knew me. They stopped me in the lobby and came to talk to me during coffee breaks. Apparently they knew all about the Tecum case and its importance.

On the second morning, I received an e-mail from the media representative at the Florida Attorney General's office. I learned that, following a complaint from the Filipino Consulate, Attorney General Bill McCollum had filed a civil lawsuit against a Miami employment service and two Boca Raton business owners and their company, alleging they advertised full-time employment and free housing but did not provide the advertised employment. The complaint further explained that the individuals took away the workers' passports and return tickets home.

Sophia Manuel and Alfonso Baldonado of Boca Raton, and their company, Quality Staffing Services Corporation and DAR Workforce Solutions USA, Inc. of Miami were named in the lawsuit for alleged deceptive employment of temporary overseas workers from the Philippines.

"These people came to Florida believing they would have a chance at the American dream of earning a decent wage to provide for their families," said Attorney General McCollum. "Instead, they were trapped in low-wage positions and have had to depend upon handouts from friends to survive because of the apparently deceptive manner in which they were recruited."

The lawsuit alleged the defendants arranged for at least thirteen and possibly as many as fifty Filipino workers to be employed full-time in food service at a Boca Raton country club from the fall of 2007 through July 1, 2008. The defendants received thousands of dollars in fees from the responding workers, who were promised free housing plus wages as part of their contracts. However, the workers discovered upon arrival that they did not have jobs at the country club and instead were sent to work part-time for $6.67 an hour at various clubs throughout Palm Beach and Dade Counties.

Additionally, the complaint alleged the "free housing" provided for the workers consisted of a three-bedroom house for twenty-five to thirty people, many of whom had to sleep on floors and even in the garage. The workers' passports were also confiscated and, despite a court order requiring Sophia Manuel to turn the passports over to the Filipino Consulate, she refused to do so which equated to contempt of a civil court order.

Under the Florida Deceptive and Unfair Trade Practices Act, the Attorney General was seeking penalties of $10,000 per violation as allowed by law, the dissolution of Quality Staffing Services Corp. and DAR

Workforce Solutions USA, Inc. and injunctions against the companies and their owners prohibiting them from engaging in any business activity or operations offering, soliciting, providing or otherwise dealing in or related to the employment of temporary workers. The complaint also named the Boca Woods Country Club Association, Inc. and Boca Woods Property Owners' Association, Inc. as the owners of the Boca Woods Country Club in Boca Raton.

I recognized right away that it sounded more like a human trafficking case than a civil matter. With my heart pounding, I made contact with the office in Florida and told them of my suspicions.

Although most of the main contacts from the Department of Justice and Department of Homeland Security were in Vienna, we had no time to waste. I called my office in Bonita Springs and Tampa Bay and advised them to get in touch with the Honorary Consul General of the Philippines in Fort Lauderdale and coordinate with them the rescue and our services. From Vienna we started coordinating the rescue, shelter and victims' services.

I couldn't believe that slavery on such a large scale had reared its ugly head. The couple involved, Sophie Manuel and Alfonso Baldonado Jr., owned the Boca Raton labor contracting service where they conspired to lure people into their employment by making false promises that never materialized. Their temporary staffing agency promised foreign workers the chance to work in the States. For a small fee they would provide a job, housing and transportation.

They had apparently started to hatch their plan years earlier. In July 2005, Manuel travelled to the Philippines and held a recruiting meeting to a captive audience of starry-eyed workers. People flocked to the event in response to several advertisements in the local newspapers about the possibilities of amazing job opportunities in America.

On that first occasion, Sophie Manuel informed them about the fortunes they could make. She dazzled them with impressive Power Point slides of rich golf courses and country clubs in and around the Miami area.

"This is where you will be working if you come on board," she told them all.

It sounded too good to be true. Of course, it was.

At least thirty-six workers signed up and parted with around $1,500 of their hard-earned money as a job security deposit.

She thanked them all and left. Subsequently no jobs came from her visit and the workers never got refunds. A few months later, and as bold as brass, the couple returned with more promises of high paying jobs that they said would guarantee at least $1,400 a month for a minimum of three years. Again workers came but this time the couple upped the stakes and took $4,000 in up-front fees from them all.

The gullible victims, all fifty of them, were desperate and in search of a better life.

This time the couple did take the workers to America, flying them in via Miami International airport on H2B guest worker visas.

Once the happy band of fifty men and women arrived, their passports were immediately confiscated. They were housed in several substandard accommodations. From the outside, the accommodation looked decent but inside it was crowded and absolutely disgusting. Their meals consisted of chicken innards or chicken feet and rotten vegetables. When one worker complained about the drinking water being warm, the water was swiftly and unbelievably replaced with Muriatic Acid. They slept on the floor of the house, some of them in the garage.

After some basic training, they were all put to work in golf and country club hotels and resorts. The couple had a contract to supply eleven such establishments with a staff of servers mostly for seasonal or supplementary work.

Then the couple dropped another bombshell when they instructed the workers there would be further "recruitment fees" and additional costs and that they would need to work to pay them off or be arrested and deported if they didn't comply.

The couple, wanting to make sure that the workers they provided were knowledgeable about things like how to set a dinner table and how to mix certain drinks, woke tired workers in the middle of the night and quizzed them endlessly on the service industry requirements. Any worker who failed the test was punished, not in a violent manner, but they were often made to go without food. If the couple received any complaints from the resorts about their workers, they were be punished in the same way.

They pushed the workers to the limit without regard to safety or health. One woman who broke her wrist and another man who started coughing up blood were refused medical attention. They were simply told to get over it and get back to work.

The victims were ordered not to leave the home under any circumstance. A neighbor stated, "I didn't see much of them. They kept to themselves. When I did, they seemed quite nice. They always waved at me and my baby."

The only time off they had off was when they were all herded into vans every Sunday and taken to the nearby church. They were forbidden to speak to anyone, though. After church they were taken home and locked up immediately. This went on for months until one of the Filipinos escaped and went to the Consul General office looking for help. The Honorary Consul General's wife went to the office of the Florida Attorney General in Fort Lauderdale and they filed the civil case.

By the time I arrived back in Florida from Vienna my team was on the verge of moving some of the victims into shelters wherever we could find enough room. There were a total of fifty Filipinos enslaved but in the end only forty-three came with us. The rest decided to stay with the couple. Two of them joined our group later on.

We were careful to keep the two married couples together. To move them all we rented three vans and moved them in small groups. When we started we soon realized we needed a bigger truck for their personal belongings. I rented a Ryder truck, but I didn't have a driver. I called one of our partners, Deputy Ed Rosado who was working with the Miami Springs Police Department and he got permission from his superiors to drive the truck for us.

Packed in like sardines, we finally made the trip from Fort Lauderdale to Southwest Florida with the rest of the victims. We arrived that night. While unloading and getting them into their assigned apartments, I took two victims and a case manager with me to the grocery store to buy food for the whole group for the entire week. We had five carts full of groceries. People were looking at us as if we were crazy!

It was easy to see that many of the victims were still traumatized, very scared and mistrusting of anyone who tried to help them in any way. They were too frightened to ask for the most basic of needs. Months after the case was over, they were still learning that they were human beings that deserved to be treated properly.

Some of the victims were taken to Sarasota. Unfortunately it was discovered that the national faith-based organization who was housing the sixteen men took them to a church and brought them in front of the congregation to let everyone know that they were newly rescued victims of human trafficking.

It caused much distress to the victims and it was a violation of the Victims Bill of Rights. The group felt horrible and uncomfortable and wanted to leave as soon as possible. One of the group members advised the case manager what had happened and also mentioned to the director that the faith-based organization had collected money from the congregation but they did not know what had happened to it. The faith-based agency had broken confidentiality and put the victims at risk—all for financial contributions.

Our staff acted as quickly as possible to get the group out. The sixteen men were split into two smaller groups. Seven of the men were taken to Clearwater while the other nine were moved to Naples where they had no further issues.

It was easy to see that since the group had gone through so much together, they were very close and very protective of each other. They had become one big family. If one victim was going through a problem or was not feeling well, the entire group was fast to help. The group dynamics were very interesting. One of the victims, Bill, who initially was the first one to escape the traffickers, emerged as the leader of the group. Bill was very giving and one of the nicest people you could ever meet. He was housed in Naples but would often communicate with the group in Clearwater to check up on them. He became the father figure for the group. If one of the others misbehaved, he would speak to them.

The case became known as Boca Thirty-nine. After about a month, I could see the group really loosening up, making more eye contact with the case managers and sharing more about the experience that they had just survived. They began smiling and just looked as though they were in a happier place.

While the case managers were working on getting the victims rehabilitated, Immigration Customs Enforcement agents were busy investigating the case. Bill told his case manager about the night that they were rescued.

"Thirteen of my colleagues had escaped... been rescued. We didn't know this at the time," he said. "The couple called a meeting and they were shouting at us, threatening us. Then I looked out the window and I could see police officers creeping up to the front door. Someone screamed and we all ran out the back door... some of our work visas had expired."

They didn't get far. They were all rounded up by the ICE agents.

"I remember," said Bill, "that the agents came in and one said loudly, that 'the group did not look like trafficking victims.'"

Of course the comment angered the case manager working with this particular group so much so that she wrote a scathing email to the agents working on the case. It provoked an email to me from their superiors. Shortly after, Bill also warned the case manager about one of the ICE agents that was investigating the case. At some point before the victims had been rescued, an ICE agent came to the home to interview a couple of workers that had left one agency and had come to this particular staffing agency. After the ICE agent left, one of the traffickers called for a staff meeting.

During the meeting, she held the ICE agent's business card and advised the entire group that the particular ICE agent was her friend and whatever she needed him to do, the agent would do. Coming from a country with a lot of corruption, the group believed her. Of course when the raid occurred, the agent was involved with the raid. The case manager advised the group she would look into it and she called the supervisor of the particular agent and advised her of what she had been told. The supervisor thanked the case manager for the information, which eventually was used in the complaint that was filed by the Department of Justice and used as evidence against the couple.

My staff worked hard to get the victims to see that the agent was not really involved with the traffickers and that it was just another lie that they had been fed. Once the group realized the truth, the floodgates opened and more information on what happened to them began to flow—the horrors of the food they were given, the punishments they received and the promises made that were broken.

A majority of the victims from the case were married with children back in the Philippines. It was very difficult for them due to the fact they had not seen their children since they had left their home, but all of them kept in touch with their families via the Internet and Web cam. I could always tell when it was seven o'clock because almost all of them would be on the computer chatting with their children before they left for school.

One of our victims named Joy had two young children and a wife back in his homeland. One night as his case manager was getting ready to leave the shelter, she found him playing his guitar and singing Barney's "I Love You" song over the Web cam to the two young children. The case manger did not say anything as she did not want to disturb the moment. I received a phone call from her later to tell me that it had touched her heart. She was still crying.

It wasn't as heartwarming for one of the married couples who had also left their two young children with relatives before embarking on their job quest to America. Since the couple was not able to send money to the family members who were caring for their children, they were told that their children would be taken to an orphanage. Upset, the couple immediately went rushing to the ICE agent working on the case. After several phone calls to high places, we were able to work something out so the children were allowed to come to the United States. It was a relief to know that this loving couple's children would be safe. The day the family was reunited was such a joyous day.

It's those moments that keep me going. The two children are now enrolled in school and learning English. They are adjusting quite well and are enjoying their time here.

There were numerous situations like that with the group that just tore my heart up, but the most distressing situation occurred with one of our male clients named Jose. Before he left the Philippines, Jose's mother became very ill. Unfortunately the family did not have the money needed for his mother's expensive treatments. When he saw the job offer in Boca Raton, he knew that it was what he needed to do to be able to make the money needed to help his mother. But because he never really earned any money to send back home for medical treatments, his mother passed away. To this day, he feels as though he let his mother down. As much as my staff and I tried to convince him that it was not true, he was still convinced he

130

was the cause of his mother's death.

During the sentencing hearing against the traffickers, Jose shared his story with the judge. Hearing the story again and seeing Jose cry in the courtroom made me, and almost everyone else in the room, cry. My hope is that one day he will realize he did do the best he could.

Not every story regarding the Boca Thirty-nine was a sad one, however. Through almost three years, there have been heart touching and funny things that have made me smile every time I think back.

One of the things that we at FCAHT do is celebrate everyone's birthday. A few weeks after the rescue, one of the victims had a birthday. The case manager went to the store and bought the biggest cake she could find. We gathered the entire group, and when the birthday boy saw the cake with his name on it, he began to weep openly. I asked him if he was okay, and he told me that it was the first time he had ever had a birthday cake. It was such an honor to have been able to share his first birthday in America as a free man.

During the birthday celebration, one of our long time volunteers was present. She immediately walked away and went to the bathroom. About ten minutes later, she came back. The volunteer explained that it was one thing to read about human trafficking, but it was another to actually meet a survivor of human trafficking. The experience overwhelmed her, but she was able to compose herself and share in the birthday celebration.

On another birthday celebration, the case manager arrived at a group's apartment with a cake only to find that they had completely moved the furniture around the apartment to make enough room for a dance area. They had a table filled with dishes that each of them had made, the lights were off and somehow they had rigged a disco ball in the apartment. The case manager just laughed as she saw how excited they were. After the case manager sang "Happy Birthday" with the group, she left so that they could continue their birthday celebration.

On another occasion, shortly after the group had been rescued, they arranged to go to a large Filipino Festival in the Tampa area. Through the assistance of the Consul's office and a wonderful pastor from a local Episcopal church, we were able to take many of them to enjoy the Filipino festivities. One of the things we quickly learned about this group was their love of boxing, basketball and wrestling. At that time, there was a wrestler with the WWE, who is half Filipino. Batista, the WWE wrestler, was a hero to many of the victims, including, Bill the leader of the group, who was actually nicknamed "mini Batista".

Towards the end of the day, there was a lot of hustle and bustle towards the seating area of the festival. I quickly found out that Batista was there. Of course our clients went crazy and immediately went to see their hero for themselves. I remember watching the clients approach him for a picture and how he gladly accepted.

Mini Batista however was very shy and got a picture taken of himself a couple feet away from his icon. It brought me a lot of joy seeing the excitement in all of their eyes when meeting Batista. I was very grateful to Batista for allowing them to have their pictures taken with him. Batista never got a chance to learn that some of the fans he was so gracious to that day were survivors of human trafficking. Batista would never know what an impact he had made in each and every one of them who got the chance to meet him.

Another thing that made it a joy working with the group was the fact they all loved to sing. Karaoke is very popular in the Philippines, which was something my staff and I learned very quickly. There were numerous occasions where we would go to the shelter, only to find them singing karaoke in their apartments. And they were all quite good with such beautiful and rich voices. Their favorite group was Journey and their favorite song was "Don't Stop Believing". They loved Arnel Pineda, since he is Filipino.

One of the younger members named Jimmy entered a singing contest and won first place. He was given the chance to sing two songs at the Tampa Bay Performing Arts Center. Although he was worried on the day of the event, he did an amazing job. I remember getting goose bumps when I heard him sing his first song. When his performance was over, the crowd chanted his name. He has become somewhat of a local celebrity within the Filipino community in the Tampa Bay area. With confidence from that experience he continues to sing at other contests and local events. I can see how much joy it brings him to be able to share his voice with so many others.

I believe the music was a powerful part in the healing process for all of them.

The Clearwater group was housed in a shelter that used to be hospital, which they all claimed was haunted. I used to enjoy my trips to Clearwater just to hear some of the things they would tell me about the building. Many of them swore they regularly heard women and children crying or asking for help. Many said they witnessed TVs and lamps turning on by themselves. One told me one night he saw a blue mist appear by the air conditioner vent and shortly after he felt pressure on his chest, as though someone had just sat on him. This obviously scared him to the point where he no longer wanted to stay in that particular room.

Another man said that he got up around five one morning to use the bathroom but as soon as he opened up the door he saw a figure standing in front of him. The first thing he thought to do was to punch the person, so he swung and nothing. There was no one there. After that, he decided not to get up in the middle of the night anymore.

The group turned to an Episcopal priest, Father Ray, who was also Filipino. He was vital in bringing peace to the group housed in Clearwater at the shelter. I am not really sure as what Father Ray did, but whatever it was, it worked, as there were no more reports from our group of scary experiences. Thanks to Father Ray, we did not have to call The Ghost Hunters.

Father Ray and his wife, Ning, did so much for the group. Father Ray offered the group spiritual counseling, and every Sunday, his wife, Ning, would use the church van to pick the group up for services. The group adored them. On his days off, Father Ray would also pick up the group and take them on fishing trips. Granted the others living in the shelter hated the fish smell in the hallway, but the group loved going on those trips.

Father Ray and his wife opened up their arms, church and home to the group, and it really helped the group see that they could still trust in people.

I cannot speak about this case without acknowledging the Consul's office. Dr. Angelo Mactangay and his wife, Mary Lou, were crucial to the case. Mary Lou was able to get the Filipino community to assist the first thirteen with housing and food. She also contacted the Florida Attorney's General office. If it had not been for that, many of them could still be in slavery today.

After the sentencing hearing of the traffickers, which didn't take place until late 2010, the Boca Thirty-nine did something none of our other clients had ever done. The group wanted to show their appreciation for every single person who assisted them along the way. The group put together a victory party. It was wonderful to meet some of the others who had helped before we became involved. We got a chance to meet the members of the Florida Attorney's General office, as well people within the community. It was a bittersweet moment for me. I was happy to see the case closed. I was happy to see the group get justice and put an end to the nightmare, but I was sad, as I knew this would be the last time I would be in the same room with each and every one of them.

Today the group is scattered throughout Florida and other parts of the United States. I am so happy to see how each and every one of them has been able to bounce back from this experience and start truly living the American dream. All of them are now working and earning money. All of them have been able to purchase a car. Some of the victims have gotten married and have started families.

Some of them are still patiently waiting for the day they can be reunited with their husbands, wives and children. It will be a special moment, especially for two of them, who left their wives pregnant and have yet to meet their daughters. Imagine meeting your child for the first time ever. It's been three long years for this group and I can't wait for the day they will be able to hug their loved ones.

Manuel was sentenced to seventy-eight months in prison; her husband, Baldonado Jr was sent away for a maximum of fifty-one months after they pleaded guilty to a number of the charges including visa fraud and making false statements to the government.

***

The Boca Thirty-nine are building new lives, free lives, and I am thrilled to see that they are now able to help others. Jimmy waited four stressful years for his T1 visa. The United States Citizenship and Immigration Service only has limited caseworkers in the state of Vermont to process T1 visas. The process was excruciatingly slow. Because of the fear that Manuel and Baldonado instilled in him of the immigration authorities, he still worried about being deported. "I am a lot better than before," Jimmy said during the long wait, "but I don't want to hide (from the ICE agents)."

His wife, who still lives in the Philippines, divorced Jimmy. She left him for Jimmy's best friend.

Jimmy works as a Certified Nursing Assistant in an Assisted Living Facility and is a valued employee. The whole building appears noticeably cleaner since he started working there. The residents are treated to frequent concerts because Jimmy is an accomplished singer. Jimmy had several public appearances in Florida, including an impromptu singing duet with a female singer where he stole the show. "I didn't even practice with the artist before we sang together," he said. When Jimmy finally received his T1 visa and work permit, we celebrated like you wouldn't believe! Jimmy came to the coalition office so happy he was crying. We took him to a restaurant for a party.

I know Jimmy appreciates the work we did for him, even though we did what we had to do—take care of fellow human beings. "I'm here because of (you and FCAHT)," Jimmy said. "I owe (you) my life! I am more than a case number."

Jimmy does his part to help the newly rescued at the shelter, paying forward the help he received. He prepares them a meal and makes them more comfortable. Gigi and I are working with him to polish up his resume so he can get a job at a hospital.

Bill settled in Las Vegas, working in the resort business at fourteen different resorts. He received his T1 visa and started the legal process to become an American citizen. He met a Filipino woman on the Internet and has big plans for his life with her

Bill was the true leader of the group. Even though he is not the oldest member, he is wise beyond his years and very levelheaded. He was the first to realize that the situation he and his colleagues were in had gone horribly wrong. He was the first one to leave and get help for everyone. Even after they were rescued and in the shelter, the others would go to Bill for advice. Bill got up in court when Sophia and Alfonso were sentenced. He looked them in the eye and said, "You don't deserve to be called Filipinos! You have shamed our country!"

In an interview, Bill, ever the spokesperson, spoke very kindly about our work. "On behalf of everyone, I am very grateful," he said. "The Rodriguez family is a model family. They have molded us as people. They helped us without expecting anything in return. Ma'am Anna, she's like my mom. She's so nice. She's a supermom!"

Joy is now saving up money to apply for permanent residency. His wife and children have finally joined him, and though finding work has been difficult, he is working.

"I think we're good," he said. "Sometimes … people want an interview and sometimes I don't want to tell them the past because it hurts us. It hurts me. The past is the past and you don't want to go back in your mind again."

Bob's family is close to joining him in the United States, but it has been a long, hard five-year wait for them. They have completed the fingerprinting process at the US Embassy. Bob is working overtime to save money to buy them plane tickets to come.

"For now I am here by myself. My kids always ask me, 'When can we be together again?' They are growing up without me."

Bob is thankful for the help he received, but he points out that he still needs support.

"Some people, after the case that I was in was over. . . I don't feel they're still around. The coalition is still giving us comfort." Father Ray has continued to be important to the Boca Thirty-nine.

"I am really thankful because he is like a father to me. He is my spiritual guide here. Sometimes I feel empty," Bob said. "I'm by myself, so every Sunday I to go to church to see him. His is a very nice person. He helps us in a lot of ways. In the Philippines, I was a Catholic, but now that I am here, I go in this (Episcopal) church."

The church has become a reunion ground for the Boca Thirty-nine. "Most of my friends, we are working different places," Bob said. "We go to church because we see each other. Now they are like my family here because I don't have any relatives here in Clearwater."

A Stroll in Mexico

My work in human trafficking has taken me to some wonderful places with incredible people. It has also taken me to some dark sordid places with dark sordid people. On one trip in particular, I crossed the border from the United States into Mexico to the "Tolerance" zone in Tijuana La Zona Norte, often referred to as la Coahulia, after one of the streets in the legal red-light district. I was with a group of undercover law enforcement officers from the United States and the Federal Police of Mexico.

Just south of the border, not far from San Diego, Tijuana, I'd been reliably informed, was a place with a dubious reputation, a place where nothing was sacred and everything and everyone could be brought at a price. All sorts of illegal activities go on there. Many of them completely out in the open while, apparently, the police force and the government turn a blind eye as long as the money keeps rolling in.

The aim of my trip was to witness firsthand the scale of the problem regarded by many as one of the major hot spots for human trafficking in the entire world, in a city where I had read young poor children got abused in the most shocking and disturbing of ways.

However it wasn't just about children getting smuggled and exploited in the country that I wanted to find out about. I also wanted to see for myself and try to understand why thousands of adults, mainly males, crossed the United States/Mexico border every day with something more sinister and evil on their minds than visiting the beautiful country.

Rumor has it that each year thousands upon thousands of Americans travel to Mexico to pay for sex with children of all ages. Web sites and adult magazines blatantly advertising sex tours to Tijuana are readily available across America. Professionally run and organized child sex package tours are widespread in Mexico, especially in the densely populated areas and in the regions with high concentrations of tourism activities.

The information about the tours I had researched didn't make pleasant reading. For around 4,000 dollars, the advertisement proudly announced in black and white, one could purchase a twelve-day sex package and enjoy "all the sex you want or have ever dreamed of." It included a limousine ride from the San Diego airport to one of the many hotels linked to the trade. It stated young children would not be supplied, but this, I'd been told, was just a front. If the price was right anything could be bought.

One national campaign against the organized child sex tourism said it simply and well, "You pay for a night; they pay with their lives."

Organized child sex rings systematically recruit children of all ages to work in pornography or the many bars or massage parlors and strip clubs in the region. Every year, thousands of vulnerable young girls and boys are lured and transported to places like La Zona to prostitute themselves, according to a child exploitation report conducted by the group, Stolen Childhood. The report outlined that an estimated 16,000 Mexican children fall prey to organized child sex tourism each year, most of them recruited or kidnapped from poor, rural cities. Corruption is evident and big business supports it while the government is apathetic to the goings-on in the sex industry.

I'd undertaken hours and hours of research on the place before I decided to step across the border. I wanted to ensure I was fully prepared for what I would find.

Tijuana was not only a city of destination for human trafficking victims but it was a popular transit city as well, often used as a springboard, propelling young, poor children into the United States for a life of sex slavery. Mexico, for a long time, has been highlighted as the number one exporter of exploited children into America. The US State Department estimated that as many as 17,000 people, primarily women and children, get trafficked into the United States to be sold as slaves of labor or commercial sexual activities each year.

Thousands of these children are introduced into a world full of indescribable nightmares. It's a breeding ground for the trafficking of young children into prostitution. For example since the early 1990s hundreds of girls and boys, some as young as ten, have been forced to cross through the San Diego/Tijuana border to be lured by local gangs into child prostitution. Across either side of the border, young children often engage in what is called "survival sex" just to ensure they have a warm meal in their bellies or a place to sleep for the night.

With all the information whirling around inside my head, I met up with the others in our group as we assembled on the US side of the border. There were eight of us all together, seven men and myself. Before we climbed aboard an old beaten up mini-bus, one of the law enforcement officers pulled at my arm. "Anna Rodriguez," he said, "'you can't go there looking like that."

I stared at him rather confused. He added, "You are well known by the pimps on that side of the border," he lowered his voice, "If they recognize you, there will be trouble and you may not be coming back… probably none of us will."

I gulped hard. I hadn't expected this. I touched the talisman hanging around my neck, one of the many I've been given over the years by victims or the family of victims who wanted me to find their loved ones. He handed me a baseball cap and a pair of large sunglasses. "These are not ideal, but it will help. Don't remove them whatever you do!"

I disguised myself as best as I could.

On the journey, he sat next to me. He warned me what I was about to witness would probably be the worst thing I'd ever seen. He advised me that reading about the place was one thing, seeing first hand was something else altogether. By the coldness of his stare, I knew he wasn't lying. He described how crime in the city was out of control due to drug and human trafficking gangs fighting against each other and the police. Murder, kidnapping, muggings, pick pocketing and gang warfare were everyday occurrences on the tough Mexican streets. He said that a few weeks earlier, the police found 1,500 shell casings on various public streets after one such episode that left thirteen suspected drug traffickers dead. In the previous year the city experienced 556 murders, mostly as a result of the escalating drug violence that has gripped the city.

I prayed God would be walking by my side and protecting me every step of the way.

We travelled the rest of the way through the rugged and dusty terrain in silence. I thought of my family and hoped I would see them again. Off in the distance I could see the large sprawling city situated on the Mexican Baja Gold coast in Baja California and could see immediately why it was considered the gateway to Mexico. There were numerous cars, buses and trucks heading in the same directions as us. No wonder it is known as the busiest border crossing in the world with the city relying heavily on its tourism trade as one of its major sources of revenue. Around 300,000 people make their way across the border every day. It's a Mecca for high school and college kids from Southern California since the legal age for drinking in Tijuana is eighteen.

It's not just legal drinking that people flock here to sample. Many products and services can be obtained at a much cheaper rate than in the United States. Everything is available—from alcohol and cigarettes to components for cars to dental work and plastic surgery. There's a massive trade in prescription drugs that can often be bought in pharmacies in the area without the need for a doctor's prescription.

We got to the area situated in the bowl of a deep valley in less than an hour. I felt very uneasy as we parked on a back street. Not to raise suspicion, we split in small groups of two. I walked slowly down a narrow lane with the officer who had given me the disguise. It seemed reasonably quiet at first. Off in the near distance I could hear loud music bellowing out from the next street over. I walked around the corner to Avenida Constitucio'n in La Zona Norte. I stopped in my tracks and stared. Bars and strip clubs lined the busy streets.

There were around five connecting streets, which I had been informed, had been designated by the government for this type of activity.

The law enforcement officer whispered for me to carry on walking.

We mingled in with the other people, mainly adult males, wandering up and down the strip or just hanging around on street corners. I could feel many of them staring at me, probably wondering why I was there. It was difficult to make out if they were johns, pimps or just regular individuals passing through.

There were also those either begging for a few dollars or trying to sell everything from drugs to flowers to switchblades to condoms. One young girl, who couldn't have been any older than seven, was walking around selling chewing gum. I hadn't seen any proof yet but I'd been informed that somewhere amongst these streets was even a considerable trade in organ trafficking mostly involving corneas and kidneys. It is a country where getting a few hundred dollars for selling body parts often replaces long-term health.

At the start of one long street we came upon a long line of prostitutes, *Las Paraditas,* as the locals called the girls who stand around waiting for business. They weren't underage children; these were older, maybe in their twenties. They were loud, streetwise and quite menacing. They grabbed out and bellowed at the men sauntering passed, *vamos al cuarto*, which meant, "Let's go to the room."

We carried on down La Coahuila. A bar owner stood in front of my colleague beckoning men into his premises. "Fresh meat… fresh young meat… twelve… thirteen… the best in town," he smiled proudly. Two gold teeth glistened in his mouth.

We hurried on as fast as we could, but I could hear him stopping someone else and going through the same routine.

On my right hand side, vans were all parked up along one side of the street with their doors open wide. As I walked past one, I noticed a TV monitor in the back and a camera pointing out of the passenger side window of the vehicles, filming what was going on across the street. I caught a glimpse of my disguised features on one of the screens as I passed.

I tried to ask my guide what was going on, but he shook his head and indicated for me to just keep moving. Next to each van stood serious looking men, with one eye on the people passing, the other watching the screens. I assumed they were the traffickers. I was wrong; most of them were enforcers, hired by the pimps and traffickers to look after their merchandise.

"Anna, look," the undercover police officer whispered to me, "There!"

I turned my head sharply and then for the first time I saw the kids. Lines of them, all ages, sizes and colors, some as young as ten, all lined up on the opposite side of the road. Boys and girls, some dressed much older. The girls wore heavy make-up, red lipstick and stood in high-heeled boots. The items most likely purchased by the traffickers to dress their merchandise up for sale and to give the impression they were older. While others stood in plaid skirts like schoolgirls. The worst thing was that these *were* just schoolgirls. The one thing they all had in common was the empty look on their faces and the dullness of their eyes—no sparkle at all.

It was then I realized why the cameras and the TVs were there in the parked vehicles. They were being used to listen in on the conversations between the johns and the kids. It was organized and profitable crime at its lowest, and the pimps weren't taking any chances on FBI agents or anyone else. The enforcers standing on the sidewalks, every ten to fifteen yards, were constantly staring and monitoring, one enforcer to every five kids and only seconds away if there was trouble.

The children appeared to be a mix of nationalities, mainly Mexican or Central American, but there were a few Asians amongst them. Then I saw a boy and a girl, around thirteen, who looked American. I wanted to talk to them, but I knew I couldn't with the enforcers so close.

The estimated average age range of children working on the streets in the city was between eleven and seventeen, which worryingly meant for every kid older than the average age, there must be one younger. I didn't want to think about it. I could imagine how the pimps had targeted the kids, knowing at that age they were impressionable, naïve and easy to control. And of course being so young they have a long and profitable shelf life to make the pimps lots of money over many years. It is reported that many are taken at such a young age that don't even remember where they came from in the first place. The life on the streets is all they have ever or will ever know.

Some of the kids appeared to have bruises on their arms and legs, I assumed caused by the pimps keeping them in line. The law enforcement officer told me this may not always be the case. "Rape," he said, "is the new thing amongst male customers." It had gotten so bad, the children now expected rape to be part of their daily lives that they were forced to endure.

"What don't the pimps stop it?" I questioned under my breath, "Or the enforcer guys?"

"They don't care," he replied as we headed down a side street. "They don't protect the children from violence from customers. They don't encourage violence. They don't want their merchandize damaged… but they wouldn't stop it as long as the price is right."

He told me about a young girl, thirteen or fourteen, beaten to death by a john in some over the top violent sex act several days before. Another boy was beaten so badly he ended up in the hospital. The drunken john told the pimp that when he'd fallen asleep the boy had tried to steal his wallet. The pimp was paid off and the man left to do it again to some other poor lost soul.

Children that should have been in school, playing soccer or going to their first dance were instead here on the street, selling their bodies or getting raped by beasts for money. I felt physically ill. I had to restrain myself from throwing up right there on the sidewalk.

"Lots of them," he added, "are probably high on drugs. The pimps get them high on drugs like crystal meth. They use it to control them, keep them from running away. Within no time they are addicted to it, and then they have them exactly where they want them. Slaving for the rest of their lives."

With tears filling my eyes and anger bubbling through my veins I watched in revulsion the situation unfolding in front of my eyes. I felt I was in some kind of movie. The children stood stationary in one place, and rarely if at all moved. One long line of them all standing in rows along one side of the street with their backs to the wall of the many bars and strip clubs or hotels.

I couldn't take my eyes off them as I slowly trudged onwards in the crowd. Then I heard the clicking noise, clicking like grasshoppers. I looked around trying to make out where the sound was coming from. Then I realized. The kids were making the noises, clicking, or hissing at us. They didn't make eye contact at all. They were making the sound to attract the attention of possible clients. Apparently there was some strange unwritten rule in the crazy place that the kids were not allowed to proposition the johns themselves, so to attract their clients, they make the clicking noise.

I briefly stopped to look at one boy, no older than twelve, dressed in a white wife-beater and tight shorts. His eyes lowered, he clicked at everyone that passed. A man approached him, after a brief conversation they walked into the door of a hotel.

I saw one young girl, no older than eleven, with her hair in pigtails, standing in a nightgown holding a little fluffy teddy bear up to her face. A fat man smirked at her and walked down the alleyway hand in hand with her. I'd had enough. I wanted to chase after him, tear his eyes out or even worse.

There were signs everywhere I looked displaying the prices of the kids for sell, special offers. Fifteen dollars got the evil, sick men fifteen minutes, but they were expected to pay another four dollars or so for the room. Condoms must be worn, but of course, intercourse without was tolerated if the price was right.

I wouldn't wish this kind of life on my worst enemy. These kids were forced to have sex continually for many hours or as long as their developing bodies could endure the strain and stress and physical abuse. There was no time off if they got sick, tired or sore. If they contracted a sexually transmitted disease, the pimp paid off the medical center to give the victim a clean bill of health. If they happened to get themselves pregnant, the girls were forced to have an abortion usually in a backroom with no proper medical equipment. They were put back out on street after a day or two.

Without making it too obvious, I shyly observed some of the pimps and the enforcers patrolling the strip. They looked to be mainly Mexican. They looked hard, ruthless, and frightening, like they would stop at nothing to get what they wanted. To me they were heartless, Godless individuals who didn't deserve to be living among decent people.

Just as bad were the hundreds of johns walking up and down the street looking for bargains as if they were walking the aisles in Wal-Mart. They made me just as sick and mad as the pimps themselves. Mexicans, Latinos, Americans in their sweatshirts and sweat pants and Japanese, many as I mentioned probably on packaged tours to the region. Some looked like your stereotypical pedophiles, but many didn't. They appeared to be all ages from late teens right up to mid-sixties and seventies, although I later found out that the average age of a perpetuator was above thirty years of age, normally single but sometimes married. They came from all walks of life. There were professionals like teachers, doctors, lawyers, as well as working class men and the unemployed. Often they are fascinated with children and children's games. They prefer them to adult-orientated activities or adult company. Many of them have child-like hobbies such as collecting popular expensive toys or keeping pets or building toy airplanes or cars.

They often surround themselves in an environment or have a place or room decorated like a children's bedroom, normally targeted to the age group they are trying to entice.

Pedophiles do the same thing as traffickers or pimps to win trust of their victims. They give them lots of attention or things their parents wouldn't allow. They build up a child's self-esteem very similar to pimps going through the grooming stage. They give them alcohol or drugs to help reduce their resistance before making their attack.

Many are addicted to porn and believe they are not doing anything wrong— that having sex with a minor is natural and even helps the child. The more I saw, the sicker I felt.

I glared at one overweight guy wearing a New York Jets T-shirt and baseball hat as he stroked a young dark skinned boy's face before leading him into a ramshackle looking hotel. He turned back and smirked before disappearing. I will never forget that man's face.

Another Mexican man walked past me leading two young girls no more than eleven down an alleyway as if he was taking his two daughters for an ice-cream cone.

The sex customers wandering the streets were endless.

If the sight laid out in front of me wasn't bad enough, it got worse. I saw a police officer standing not far from us, handing out pieces of paper. I walked towards him, determined to tell him what I had just seen. I picked up one of the flyers by my feet. My mouth fell open; I physically wobbled. The flyer wasn't trying to prevent crime; it was promoting it. Printed on the paper were the innocent faces of young children. Alongside each face was a price and a list of things they "liked" to do. It was like a catalogue, maybe thirty kids on it. At the bottom it gave directions to a hotel where even younger children could be found.

The undercover officer reluctantly told me that the kids were the veterans; the "young meat" could be found on the second floors of the buildings that surrounded us where *babies* who were sold for oral sex, for big money.

Young kids! Babies! Surely hell couldn't be as bad as this. This was so, so wrong. When God created heaven and earth I don't think even he could ever had envisioned anything so depraved, so depressing. Animals didn't behave like this. It was inhuman. And with a local police station right at the center! Police officers blindly walked by the children as though they were invisible. An entire culture ignored what was going on due to the amount of profit that could be made.

I was told government officials were on the pimp's payroll. There were rumors of police officers earning double their wages by helping the pimps control and grow their business.

To meet the growing demand for fresh, young and new faces there is a great need for the sex traffickers to effectively supply the sex industry with children. The traffickers, sex tourist operators and everyone else involved in the shameful trade know that there is a huge demand for young children and they will often pay hundreds and sometimes thousands of dollars when children are especially young.

As I walked on, head bowed, I heard a loud slapping noise as I saw one of the enforcers march across the street and hit a young girl full force across her face. Like me, everyone stopped and turned to watch. He yelled at her, and then he marched off, leaving her bruised, still standing in a doorway. Everyone continued on, except for me. It was heart wrenching. I stepped towards her, to give her something, maybe some money. Suddenly I felt the barrel of a gun in my lower back.

Muevanse. "Move on," someone hissed at me. I went to turn around but the butt pushed in tighter to my skin.

I was too stunned to actually put one foot in front of the other, but the undercover law enforcement officer came to my rescue. He grabbed my hand.

"Anna… keep moving… don't look back," he whispered and then more or less dragged me out of the street.

My heart beat in my chest; my legs turned to jelly. I couldn't even speak. I wanted to get out of this place. As far away as I possibly could. I felt dirty, and I wasn't even the one being abused.

I burst out crying, started hyperventilating and didn't stop until long after we crossed back across the border. I felt so powerless! I'd been driven out of town by gunpoint. There was nothing I could have done to save these children.

When I got home I was simply too distressed to tell my husband what I had seen and what I had gone through. I went straight to bed, crying myself to sleep. I didn't sleep long. I tossed and turned until I got up and cried some more. I felt like I betrayed those kids. Why didn't I do more for them? At the same time I knew that I could do nothing for them. I probably wouldn't be here today if I had tried anything more.

It had been so hard leaving those children in a place like that, knowing I should have taken them all with me. When I closed my eyes I could see their faces, the girl with the fluffy toy, the boy getting his hair smoothed by one of those creatures.

Even to this day, that day probably more than anything still haunts me, shocks me. These weren't children anymore, just bodies, empty shells with no life, no smiles, and no future. I still can't understand how children can be sold as pieces of meat for the greed of money. It was so hard to see US citizens going across the border to have sex with young girls and even boys.

I wanted to go back, but I was cautioned against it. Sources told me I was lucky to get out the first time; it would be madness to do it again. I felt powerless as one person. It's such a big problem that involves governments, education, cutting off the demand and stopping the supply.

The government of Mexico needs to take action and go to war against the people involved so they can save their children. The governments and the people of every other country including the United States need to take action against the monsters who demand this of our kids and the monsters that make money from the misery. More forces and funds should be allocated to end such crime against humanity.

We must all come together and put aside any differences or territorial wars and think about the victims. We must also understand that human trafficking is a Global issue and it includes the United States Yes! We have victims in the United States, and we keep turning our backs to them.

In the Bowels of the Super Bowl

After the nightmare I witnessed in Mexico I was extremely depressed. For the umpteenth time, I considered quitting. I felt I was barely making a dent in the horrors being done to humans by other humans, and the emotional stress and strain of time away from my children was extremely difficult.

But once again I was re-energized in 2007 when my daughter Gigi decided she would like to follow in my footsteps and join the crusade. She sat down with me one night in my kitchen and opened her heart up to me. "Mom, I can see the passion you put into your work." She held my hand. "All the stories you have told us about the victims… I would like to feel that same passion in my job… I want to find out more about all the great things you do."

A part of me wanted to tell her to forget it, go do something else with her life. But the other half was thrilled to pieces. After completing the legal documentation and an intensive training program, Gigi became the newest member of the Florida Coalition against Human Trafficking. She set up camp in the new Clearwater office with the aim of helping me to move that part of the business forward.

From day one she did an amazing job, very conscientious, extremely hard working, if I do say so myself. Within no time at all she began to develop an outstanding program for victim services in the area and took a lot of pressure off me. I worked her very hard indeed because I didn't want anyone to say she only got the role because she was my daughter and she didn't deserve it.

One of the first cases she got involved in was the rescue of a young Haitian girl who had been identified as human trafficking victim. Georgina was referred to us by ICE in Fort Lauderdale and was transported to our shelter and met by one of our case managers. Georgina walked in to the room in a white blouse, black dress with matching shoes and dark rimmed glasses. When I met her a while later she came across as very shy and timid; she kept apologizing all of the time and her eyes looked as if she was about to burst into tears.

She was recruited back in Haiti twelve months earlier by a Haitian doctor who was about to open an office in Fort Lauderdale. Like thousands of human trafficking victims, she was promised her a better life in Florida and the chance to make lots of money. She had no medical assistant experience, but the doctor said he would personally train her and she didn't need to worry.

"I was so excited to be going," she told me, "I'd never been to America before. My family was so proud the day I was leaving… I felt like a movie star."

With the doctor's contacts, she got a visa to work in the United States without much trouble soon after they arrived in Fort Lauderdale.

"At first everything went well. The job was hard and a lot to remember, and lots of paperwork, but I soon got used to it."

She wriggled in her chair, rubbing her arms as if they were irritating her. I noticed bruising on her legs and what looked like a bite mark on her arm just below her elbow.

"What happened then?" I looked across at the frail girl.

"Well," the girl voice lowered, "'He started touching me…. he was always behind me… close to me."

She went quiet. I let her compose herself.

"One afternoon after the last client left, he forced me to have sex with him," she began to cry. "I fought him, but he hit me, slapped my face. I didn't want him to hurt me… in the end I just lay there…."

She went on to tell us in detail how he raped her every night. Sometimes he would close early just so he could have sex with her. She became his sexual servant and his domestic slave. He also had her working at his office doing other chores and not what she was promised. If she didn't comply, he threatened her with immigration.

"He would hit me and kick me every day. He bit me and burned me with cigarettes… look." She showed me the multiple scars all over her body, legs and her arms. Some scars were so deep that they will be with her for the rest of her life.

"And because of him, I wear these," she fiddled with her glasses, before removing them. "He beat me so often on my head I lost some of my eyesight in my left eye." She looked at the desk. "I didn't need glasses before he… before he…" she didn't finish the sentence. She laid her head on the desk and sobbed. I'm not ashamed to say I did, too.

After a tortuous six months, Georgina finally escaped from his clutches after running away one day when he was out of town on business. She headed to the local police station. Thankfully they believed her story. The doctor was arrested but rather than the case being prosecuted under federal law, they decided to charge him under state law. He received a sentence of time served. Due to a lack of understanding and knowledge about human trafficking, the court system ended up re-victimizing a victim that went through hell. No justice was served.

Georgina now works in a large hospital. She's made lots of new friends who are there to support her.

Just like me when I first met Chica, Gigi went through every range of emotion while involved with Georgina. My daughter couldn't stop talking about the case, day and night and just couldn't believe how a respectable doctor could treat anyone so badly. It made her even more determined to grow and succeed into the role.

Coincidently a week after Georgina's case went to trial, I received another call about another Haitian girl who was in need of our assistance. Josephine was referred to me by a Catholic Charities staff member from Orlando. Our Tampa office received a call from a man from Catholic Charities who had just received a phone call from a homeless shelter in Melbourne, Florida, to say they had a Haitian girl with her newborn baby and that she was a victim of human trafficking. The man said she had been dropped off at their office by another human trafficking agency in South Florida who said they didn't have any more funding to support her.

"We have no facilities here," Tom from Catholic Charities said over the phone. "No shelter and no services for Josephine and her child. I was praying that you would take her."

Of course when I heard that I was shocked, not just about the girl and her baby but also that another agency had just dropped her off with no referrals to another agency that could continue her care. It made me mad to think we had so many agencies in the area and none of them worked together in times like this. Many of the new agencies springing up had no experience and had no clue about victim's services or human trafficking.

Putting my frustration aside, I immediately arranged to have one of our case managers from Tampa drive almost three hours to Melbourne to pick up Josephine and her six-month-old child and then drive five hours to get them to one of our safe houses in southwest Florida.

Meanwhile I got our team to call and get donations of clothing and baby furniture and get the one bedroom apartment in one of the complexes furnished and ready for their arrival. Most of the furniture was donated by Good Samaritan and some was purchased by us. It was amazing how much help and support we got from One Way Out Ministries in Fort Myers. And it was great to see other survivors living at the apartment complex help by putting the crib together and other things just to welcome Josephine and her baby.

They arrived from Melbourne at ten that night, and when she saw her apartment she started crying. "Is this my place?"

"Yes," I said, "This is your new home."

She hugged all of us and thanked us for taking her out of the shelter and bringing her into a place where she could be safe and happy with her child.

The next day, we interviewed her. She had been adopted in Haiti by a family and brought to the United States. She was not allowed to go to school and became the domestic slave of the family. She wasn't beaten or forced to have sex with anyone, but she was their slave, not allowed to leave or go out, and made to work all day and night for no money. One morning when the family was out, she escaped and stopped someone in the street who took her to the agency.

The case was referred to as a *restavec* case. A *restavec,* from the French phrase, *one who stays with*, was a child in Haiti who was sent by their poor parents to work for another household as a domestic servant. In some cases, the child is treated well. However, in other cases, the child can be abused and treated like a slave. With all the disasters Haiti has experienced over the last few years, there seems to have been an increase in this activity and evidently traffickers have seized the opportunity presented by all the grief and desperation to lure or abduct children away from the island.

After the investigation and the trial, Josephine's traffickers were found guilty, and she was granted compensation.

As the case manager started working with Josephine, we realized that she had not received any type of services, like counseling, from the other agency. We had to start from scratch. Within six months, she started working in a local store while her baby attended day care. In no time she was a different person. She successfully transitioned out of our program and today has her own place and is working full time, and her daughter is doing really well at school.

In 2009, we teamed up with several other groups when we became involved in one of the biggest fights against human trafficking ever.

The Super Bowl, to most Americans, is the greatest sporting event on earth—an occasion where millions of fans sit back and watch some of the finest athletes in the world pit their muscle and brains in the ultimate sporting contest.

Before I got involved in human trafficking, I always loved watching the Super Bowl, and I would never have imagined that below the surface of all the glamour and the glitz, there was an underbelly of human trafficking taking place on a grand scale. As the crowds flock into the hosting city to see the game, so do the pimps, with their girls, many of them minors, to satisfy the huge demand for sex and drugs.

I heard about the crazy things that went on at these events while I attended conferences around the country. It was a magnet for pick pocketing, bets, scams, counterfeit merchandise, and prostitution.

One evening, a few weeks before the Super Bowl took place in Tampa in 2009, I was having dinner with Brad Dennis from KlaasKids and a few other people. When the conversation turned to the event and all the illegal activities surrounding it, we decided to use the crowds and the publicity to educate people about human trafficking as it was happening right under their noses.

The Florida Coalition against Human Trafficking partnered with KlaasKids Foundation and fifty-five community volunteers to address the influx of potential traffickers and their victims in and around the area during the Super Bowl.

Each of the partner agencies played a part in the development and execution of the weeklong outreach program. FCAHT provided critical funding, paying for all the outreach materials. T-shirts with the *Tackle the Trafficker* logo, which was designed by my son, Rob, were printed by a T-shirt company in Pensacola.

FCAHT also funded travel and hotel accommodations for Brad Dennis from KlaasKids. The KlaasKids Foundation provided lots of the planning, logistics and coordination efforts for the outreach and information concerning area missing children. The police were also involved, along with Stand Up for Kids, Free International, Global Child Rescue plus many others. It took some organizing and lots of talking, sometimes arguments, but in the end we pulled it together.

We had teams working day and night in and around the area. We walked the street, dressed in our bright orange *Tackle the Trafficker* T-shirts that demanded a halt to child sex trafficking. We carried out small training sessions and sometimes just stopped and talked to people. We tried to create an informal presence and not get in people's faces. The media response was tremendous and provided a counter-point to the area's leading alternative newspapers that featured the cover story "Super Blow… it's all about Sex, Drugs and How you Roll."

Our first command center was the Emmanuel Church in Clearwater. The second day we moved the command center to space at the Salvation Army on Sligh Avenue in Tampa. The weeklong event helped to develop a spirit of teamwork amongst the partner groups, law enforcement and the community. It was great to see people working together. It was all about the victims.

Two weeks prior to the Super Bowl in Tampa, law enforcement conducted prostitution sweeps across the city. But we soon found out that the commercial sex operation went completely underground. The pimps moved their business to the Internet.

We had a bank of computers set up researching the Web sites promoting this type of activity. What was interesting was that we had more collaboration from the FBI than from the law enforcement local task force.

Groups of volunteers on foot walked the different locations near the stadium, Clearwater and St. Petersburg. During the day teams patrolled from early morning until the evening, educating business owners about human trafficking. Overnight, from nine p.m. until five a.m., other groups took to the street for outreach, searching for potential victims.

We carried a sheet of talking points to use if we spotted suspected victims.

OUTREACH TALKING POINTS:

- Representing the Florida Coalition Against Human Trafficking
- Conducting outreach to educate people about human trafficking and specifically sex trafficking that may occur due to big events.

POTENTIAL INDICATORS of sex trafficking or the use of minors for sex are:

- Presence of an overly controlling and abusive "boyfriend" or "daddy"
- Constant traffic in & out of hotel room
- Presence of apparent bodyguard, "look-out"
- Numerous girls in hotel room (controlling male or female figure with them)
- Inability or fear to make eye contact (Demeanor—fear, anxiety, depression, submissive, tense, nervous)
- Injuries/signs of physical abuse or torture
- Restricted/scripted communication
- Claims of being an adult although appearance suggests adolescent features
- Girls with excess amount of cash
- Several hotel room keys
- Signs of branding (tattoo, jewelry)
- Lying about age/false identification
- Inconsistencies in story
- Trashcans with numerous condoms, lubricants etc.

Walking the streets looking for victims proved quite scary. We knew any kind of confrontation with the pimps could be dangerous. Many pimps carry weapons, and we knew they wouldn't think twice about using them. The message to our team was *don't be a hero.*

By the Tuesday of Super Bowl week we started to see some activity picking up as the media circus and fans started to arrive into town. It wasn't long before Super Bowl parties began springing up all over the place. Along with the genuine fans came the pimps and thousands of prostitutes, strippers and pole dancers. Many of the girls hiding behind the short skirts and push-up bras were in fact young children and victims of human sex trafficking.

The Super Bowl always proved to be one of the biggest human trafficking events in the United States, and now I could see why.

I saw cabs hired for the week by the pimps so the vehicles could be turned into mobile brothels. These cabs patrolled up and down the street every few minutes or so.

The nights were long. I slept for a whole week on a sofa at a Ministry program home. There were eight to fifteen of us sleeping at that facility. Thanks to the community, we were provided with meals every day. They were very nice to us.

After three days, we were all so tired from going to bed at four or five in the morning and waking up early the next day. The accommodation was noisy and difficult to get any proper sleep because people were always coming and going. It was getting to me. I was frustrated from what I saw and tired from lack of sleep.

I was working in a group of four, three of us ladies and a man named Brad. After a few days we became known as "Brad's Angels" like the seventies TV show *Charlie's Angels*. One of the partners got us hats that said "Angels". It made our day and gave us energy to continue for two more days.

The entire week was eye opening. It proved to me that there was a real seedy side to events like this, with lots of demand and unfortunately the supply on tap to satisfy those vile demands. Due to the success, we partnered again for the 2010 Super Bowl in Miami. We eventually went to Super Bowls in Arlington, Texas, and Indianapolis, Indiana, too. Out of all the four, Miami topped the lot. It was amazing and sad at the same time. Miami had all the fuel for corruption. There were drugs, girls and sex. Twenty-four hours a day for a whole week.

When we decided to do another outreach we notified local groups in the Miami area who were interested in fighting human trafficking or who assisted sexually abused victims and asked them to join us. We explained to them what we had done in Tampa. We wanted to be sure that they didn't think that we were invading their city. We welcomed their help.

The Florida Coalition against Human Trafficking again partnered with KlaasKids for this event. The hotels are so expensive during a Super

Bowl, we didn't want to use our funds to spend that kind money for a hotel. Instead we were allowed to stay in a gym, with nearby showers in a church. FCAHT funded the whole operation. We were sleeping on air mattresses and sleeping bags. We provided the volunteers with a continental breakfast, sandwiches and some dinners. The coalition paid for the T-shirts and all outreach material. We wanted to show them our gratitude for taking time from their families to help us out.

Kristi House, Stand Up for Kids, and Free International also joined in as our partners. Volunteers came from Oregon, Alabama, a church from Fort Myers, One Way Out Ministries and others. We had 164 volunteers.

Our volunteers started the day around nine each morning. We would assign the areas we wanted them to cover. We provided them a bag with all the printed materials they would hand out and then sent them out. We would also go out and do outreach with them. We would return to the command center, which was at the church, and we would debrief the groups. Based on the information we got back, we would prepare lead information to forward to law enforcement. One of the leads that we received during the day was that a man had checked into a hotel with a teenage girl. Law enforcement later followed up that night and arrested the man who had brought a fourteen-year-old girl from Hawaii and was prostituting her. The girl was rescued.

After we returned from the day shift, we would pull out our air mattresses, which we had leaned against the walls, and take a nap until six o'clock. We would have a quick dinner. Then immediately we would drive to South Beach and would work there from nine p.m. until four or five in the morning. We targeted the South Beach area because it was the location of all the Super Bowl parties, according to the Internet postings for sex. At night, we broke down into groups of three or four people and just started walking around. We would look around to see if we could identify any pimps that were with minors.

I saw pimps stopping girls on the street and trying to recruit them in broad daylight. I spent time walking the street and listening to snippets of conversations between pimps and their girls.

On one patrol, my colleagues and I walked slowly down one of the main street. It was still buzzing with loads of people looking for bars and hanging around on the corners around two in the morning. Near the corner of Fourteenth Street and Washington Avenue in South Beach, I heard a female crying and a male screaming at her at the top of his voice.

"You do as I say," he pushed her up against a shop window.

We stopped to keep an eye on the situation by pretending to be looking for activity around the area.

"You told me we were going to be here for a party. You never told me I would have to sell my body," she pleaded.

He squeezed her face, grabbing her arm. She yelled in agony. "You are here to do whatever I tell you! Now shut the f**k up!"

She kept crying. "'But I'm tired... Please. Let me go home."

He pushed her again, knocking her to the ground. I wanted to help, but I knew it was dangerous. Sticking out of the top of his trousers was the pistol grip of a gun.

"Now clean yourself up," he spat his words at her. I slyly took a photograph on my cell phone camera, careful he didn't see what I was doing. In the photo you could see in the girl's face how scared she was. The pimp turned around and stared at me. I pretended to look at the poster in the display.

My colleague walked around the corner and called for help but the police were busy with another incident. They soon sent a patrol car to assist us. The officer that responded used his emergency lights and siren, though. The pimp heard the siren and looked at us, and he grabbed the female by her hair and forced her inside a waiting taxi and took off. When the police officer arrived, it was too late. I felt so angry; I had let him take her. I wanted to follow them, but I knew I couldn't have done much more than what we had done.

In the church gym where we slept, the air conditioning didn't work properly. We were very hot and sweaty. Our breakfast consisted of donuts and coffee. They were not very healthy, but delicious all the same after a long night walking the streets.

The facility only had three showers. We had two bathrooms for male and female with their own showers. At first there were only eight of us staying at the church but the last two nights we had over sixty turn up. In order to have hot water to shower I had to get up by six in the morning have a shower and then go back to sleep for another hour before all the volunteers showed up at nine. The size of our group grew as well. We had 168 volunteers doing street outreach at its peak.

Again the plan was to turn up at the Super Bowl in Miami and be out on the street before the big game, scouting for children-turned-sex workers. Identify and rescue, was our refrain.

We would use the insights we had gained the previous year to spot underage boys and girls being used in trafficking.

Outreach started early on the Tuesday morning before right up to the Saturday night before the Super Bowl event took place on Sunday. Super Bowl Sunday was the day to pack up and return home to sleep for the rest of the day.

Just the amount of people turning up for the event was amazing. There seemed to be everlasting parties going on the beach or in hotels and bars. At times, the smell of marijuana was so strong I found myself walking closer to the waterfront into the fresh air so I wouldn't get a contact buzz. There was also a lot of drinking going on, young boys below the legal age drinking beer. I saw a pimp stopping a couple of rich looking girls outside a bar. He was trying to sell them drugs. He had a bag with him full of different tablets and substances. They brought something off him, and they went separate ways.

In South Beach between Collins and Washington Street I walked through an active track. In this track we saw more than thirty girls. It reminded me of the streets in Mexico where all the girls were lined up on one side and their pimps on the other side of the road. In some areas there were parking garages where the girls stood, while on the fourth floor opposite, the pimps sat watching their stable and making sure the girls were working. A girl would take a client up the elevator of the parking garage and ten minutes later they would come back down, the girl back to her assigned track and the client shuffling off.

On Washington Street there were so many strip clubs. The girls paraded up and down the sidewalk, barely dressed, promoting the strip club. On Washington Street in Miami, there was the Madonna Strip Club. The girls were wearing very little clothing, almost out on the sidewalk in front of the business trying to attract male customers to come inside. I saw some families with their children walking by and covering the kids' eyes.

The Super Bowl is a family event, and children should not have to observe this type of behavior.

Early Thursday morning, around four, we saw a very young girl, probably around fifteen, being dragged out of a nightclub by four guys. She was struggling and fighting the guys off. One of the guys used his finger to break her pantyhose and started touching her private parts.

"Stop that!" I shouted.

A barrage of verbal abuse came back at me from the men. One carried on, trying to kiss the girl, while another one groped her. They were taking her toward the parking lot where all the pimps were and where all the sexual activity was taking place.

"I'm going to call the police," I warned them.

They all stared at us, before walking away up an alleyway.

We raced over to comfort the poor girl. She was crying and trying to cover herself up. It was easy to see she was under the influence of some type of drug. Her eyes were rolling back; she was slurring her words, almost falling to sleep where she stood.

"Are you okay?" I asked her.

"Yeah, she's fine," one of the men shouted back.

She could barely talk. My colleague, Brad Dennis, held her up to keep her from falling on the sidewalk while I took off running and looking for the cops. I found two police officers. They followed me back to the girl. She was taken to the hospital and later her family contacted. It appeared she was under the influence of Rohypnol, known commonly as the date rape drug. It wasn't the first or last time that drug was used that week. That girl was one of the lucky ones.

Most nights I saw pimps driving around in large black SUVs with girls on the top promoting the fact there was "pussy available" and the name of some club. Then there were large trucks with glass sides where girls would parade behind the glass enticing men to step inside. Then the vehicles would park. One night, I saw a famous Hollywood actor step inside one of these mobile lap-dancing trucks with a few other men. He was standing in the pimp-mobile sipping champagne when the door was locked behind them. I waited for almost one hour for him to come back out. But he stayed inside much longer.

On Saturday night before the big game, I was standing behind a gang of young girls walking the street without their parents. They were all dressed in a way to attract attention to themselves. A pimp in a limo glided up to them and started sweet talking them. "You are beautiful. I can make you my queen and take good care of you."

The girls giggled and carried on.

"You will love my kingdom." His lines were so corny it seemed impossible not to see through them. "Come on… come for a ride." The girls stopped, and still chatting with each other, took a step towards the vehicle.

I walked up to the girls and started up a conversation. I said: "Hey, we're visiting here. Can you tell me where I can get a good burger?"

The pimp looked at me and spat on the ground. He was angry and tired of waiting and he got into the car and sped off.

"Girls," I said to them, "Whatever you do never go with a man like that." I explained all about the victims and pimps. By the end the young girls were crying and thanking me for saving them.

We were able to disrupt a couple of others from being recruited by the pimps, but on other occasions we were too late because the girls got inside the pimps' vehicles and rode away with them.

It was exhausting work, walking the streets and handing out leaflets

We had to keep our wits about us at all time. One of my colleagues was spat at, another pushed to the ground by a pimp who purposely barged past her as she went to the aid of a young girl getting abused on the street by a gang of men.

The first few days of the outreach program a major news channel followed us around filming us. While the film crew was with us, we had a great turnout of volunteers including another anti-trafficking agency in Miami that joined our efforts. Once the film crew left, the volunteers and the agency never came back. It was all about being on TV and not the cause.

We were happy with what we were able to achieve. We got our message across to several hundred people. It proved agencies could operate together without the infighting. We had many leads regarding missing children and several children were discovered. And there were several instances of "direct intervention;" resulting in several females being removed from potentially dangerous situations, and at least three females were protected from potential pimp recruitment.

During Super Bowl 2011 in Arlington, Texas, we were invited to assist and coordinate outreach by Traffick911. We had 224 volunteers and we stayed at the Ministry Hall at the University of Texas at Arlington. My bed for a week was a sofa.

Even the airline industry collaborated, with flight crews distributing materials on flights about trafficking and how to spot it. There was a campaign by Traffick911 called I'm *Not Buying It!* supported by sixty nonprofits and faith-based groups. Various football stars made public service announcements entitled "Real men don't buy children. They don't buy sex."

That year we had volunteers from Alabama, Oregon, Nevada and Texas. Due to sleet and snow, yes sleet and snow in Texas, we could not do much street outreach as the roads were closed. But we had great success monitoring the Web sites.

We noticed that due to the media attention given to some groups also doing outreach, a lot of the activity went underground. It was a media circus! We were not happy with these other organizations that were using the event for their own personal and fundraising agendas. Groups were present that had never been in Tampa or in Miami who were making a huge public display. It was frustrating to us and an eye opener.

I was only able to get outside and do a couple of outreaches because of the weather. One early morning around one, I was out riding in a van, as always paying attention to my surroundings. I saw this girl all by herself, but she was really beautiful. She was standing right in front of a Mexican store. I asked the driver of the van to make a right turn. I jumped out of the van and I told the driver, "Go inside the store and just buy whatever you want, a soda or something."

I walked up to her. "Oh my God! We're here for the Super Bowl but we're so bored because of the snow and the sleet. We're trying to find a place where we can dance to some Latin music," I said. When she started talking, I immediately realized, "This is a guy!" I was talking to a transvestite.

He explained, "Oh, you're in the wrong area. You shouldn't be here. This is mostly prostitution. You need to go more toward the downtown area. That's where you're going to find the places that are more suitable for you." He started giving me the names of the best places.

"By the way," I asked, "since you said that this is an area where there is a lot of prostitution, is it females or transvestites? Because I know that you are a transvestite."

"Thank you for treating me with respect," he said. Nobody treats me with respect."

I told him that I respect everybody and that I was also there looking for missing kids that have run away from home, thinking that they might be in areas like this.

"Oh honey!" he said. "Those kids are my competition. They have pimps and the pimps are putting them to work. And because they are young and tender, they are more in demand. So I'll help you! If you go to this cantina, you're going to find a lot of kids that you're looking for."

Now I talk with transvestites whenever I can. I always treat them with respect and carry on a conversation with them. They are always willing to help me and tell me what I'm looking for.

In 2012, the Super Bowl was in Indianapolis. It was the same scenario as Arlington. We had about thirty volunteers. There was another media circus that again pushed the pimps underground. When a law enforcement agency does a raid, they are very secretive. They certainly don't call the media to advertise what they are doing. They wait until they complete the operation and then they send out a press release. Are they going to let the bad guys know ahead of time what they are doing? No! It was disappointing!

In Indianapolis we stayed in a missionary church that had a day care. It was an old building, built in 1928. It had four floors with a basement. We were on the third floor. On one side of the building there was a private dorm with bunk beds one, two three high. This side of the building was for females. On the opposite side was the same thing for males. Each area had shower rooms. At the end of the hallway was a kitchen. The members of the community were feeding us on a daily basis. They were bringing soups and beef stew and salads and stuff like that. They served breakfast for us.

They set up tables for our computers and they had Wi-Fi for us. We looked at the postings so we could map out an area where the postings were coming from and the area of the main events for the Super Bowl parties.

One night we went out. It was cold but no snow. This time I was hitting the Hispanic places. I was about two blocks off from the main party area. We had information about a Mexican Restaurant that would have dancing after they closed the restaurant. We heard that this was a place where minors would hang out.

As we were leaving this restaurant and walking back toward Super Bowl village, we saw this young girl with two other girls and three boys. She was stumbling and her friends were holding her up or she would have fallen for sure. One of the other girls was calling her: "Bitch!" and pushing her. A boy was trying to touch her butt.

In my group were three females and a male, I stopped. Everyone stood there and looked at me. I said, "It's fine let's stay here for a minute. It looks like a disturbance right there." When you do outreach, you have to be open-minded, you can't just concentrate on one thing. So out of the blue, this girl literately dropped to the ground.

I immediately ran to the girl and asked, "Are you okay, sweetie? Are you okay?" Her eyes were white, rolled back in her head. I told one of the guys, "Just try to flag down the first cop that you see." We had seen all these cops in Super Bowl village, now we weren't seeing a one. Like the old saying, where is a cop when you need one? The other girls with this girl were trying to brush me off saying, "Oh she's fine! She's fine. She just had a little bit to drink."

I asked, "How could she be drinking? Indianapolis has a minimum age for drinking. They got all really nervous. The female that was pushing her and one of the males took off running and disappeared.

Finally a police car drove up. My team was waving to them. The officers lifted the girl up. Then the girl became very violent with the cops. She was screaming and kicking at them. They hand cuffed her and were going to take her away. I suggested to them that they should take her to the hospital. I explained to them what we had observed. I do not know what was going to happen to this girl had we not stopped but at least I know that she was taken care of.

Although hard work and shocking at times, again it proved a great success. We only had fifty-five volunteers in Tampa; in Miami we had 168 and 224 in Arlington a year later and thirty in Indianapolis. In Miami in total fourteen leads were generated regarding missing children;

and six children were recovered. There were twenty-three direct contacts of potential commercial sexual exploitation victims occurred. Five specific leads regarding potential commercial sexual exploitation victims activity were passed on to law enforcement and four leads regarding potential commercial sexual exploitation victims activity were relayed to the law enforcement juvenile sweep team. Numerous instances of direct intervention resulted in several females removed from potentially dangerous situations, and many females prevented from potential pimp recruitment.

After my experiences, I will never look at a big sporting occasion quite the same. As one colleague said, not only is the Super Bowl the biggest sports event of the year, it's also the biggest human trafficking event of the year. The Super Bowl and large events draw traffickers to bring their "merchandise". It could be sex trafficking or labor trafficking victims. The Super Bowl is not exempt from this type of activities.

***

We do quite a bit of outreach in an interesting area of Orlando known as the Orange Blossom Trail, often referred to as the OBT. While the name may sound idyllic and picturesque, seedy is a better description. We focus our outreach in this area during the Florida Classic, an annual college football game between the Bethune-Cookman University Wildcats and the Florida A&M Rattlers. The prostitution business in Orange Blossom Trail is booming during the weekend of this football match-up.

Our outreach programs have a two-pronged goal. The volunteers pass out pamphlets for public awareness, and they also are looking for underage victims of prostitution. If a possible minor victim is located, law enforcement is called in to affect a rescue.

At night, you see girls walking on the street, never with a purse. They carry a cell phone. On one side are the girls; on the other, the pimps. Guys riding bicycles up and down the street are the enforcers.

The area is full of minors. There are strip clubs all along the road. There is a section where the transvestites work. There is a section with black prostitutes. There's an area for gays and lesbians. As you get closer to the mall, the prostitutes are white and underage. You also see law enforcement driving up and down the road, but they don't do anything.

Right next to the McDonalds, which is a family restaurant, is a major chain economy motel. You see the car drive up, the guy go in. And ten minutes later, you see a girl come out of the room spitting. A marquee advertising a strip club in the area even boasts that it has fourteen beautiful girls and one ugly girl! It is disgusting the amount of activity in this area.

The first year we did the Florida Classic, I saw a young girl as I was scanning the Internet postings. I said, "Oh my God! This is a minor! Definitely a minor." I submitted the information to the law enforcement agency that night.

The next morning, I called to make sure they received it. The officer said, "No, I haven't read it yet, but let me open it now." When he saw the picture, he agreed. "That picture definitely looks young," he said. "We're going to check into it now."

I was out doing outreach with Gigi, and we had stopped at the motel the girl was working at when the officer called me back. "Anna, we got her! We got her!" he said. "Where are you?" he asked, just as I turned to see him coming out of a room.

"I'm right here!" I said

The girl was eighteen and from Dallas, but she was posting pictures of herself at sixteen. She went back to live with her mom, but unfortunately, within two months, she was back on the streets. We can only do so much. We can't force people to take what we are offering. I

This outreach, people don't understand it. My adrenaline gets pumping and I stay out all night. People ask me, "What were you doing in the OBT until five in the morning?"

I tell them, "I was trying to identify and rescue potential victims!"

The volunteers don't always get it either. I always tell volunteers, "Do not get out of the car!" What did one guy do? He saw a girl getting beat up and got out of the car. The pimp got right up next to the girl, pulled up his shirt and showed off his gun to the guy. This scared the volunteers, of course. I was livid that night.

Welcome to America

More than twenty-one million people are victims of human trafficking. Quite a shocking statistic to say the least; yet to be honest, that number felt as if it related to the Florida area alone with its rapid growth in construction, agriculture and manufacturing and, of course, its huge draw for tourism. Florida is the perfect breeding ground for widespread human trafficking operations.

Trafficking spread through Florida like a cancer. Our office was inundated with phone calls and messages about possible wrongdoing all over the state on a daily basis. With the number of cases we were beginning to uncover, I was sure it wouldn't take long until we ranked right up there with California as the number one state for modern-day slavery. That is not really a record to boast about!

The need for education intensified daily. We needed to tell the public about the horrors of human trafficking and teach them how to recognize it. Due to our proactive approach in the community, we find leads on potential victims and refer them to law enforcement. We go out and find victims. The victims are not going to come into an office, and they certainly aren't going to walk into a police station to say they are victims and need help. These are the "invisible victims." We have to identify them. We have to get out into the streets and find them.

Then once we identify the victim, we must identify the perpetrator and do what we can to help the law enforcement agency bring them to justice. That part of the process often is long, and in lots of cases, the traffickers get away with it because of massive loopholes in the legal system.

That is disappointing, but our main priority is always to rescue the victims as soon as possible. If we get the evil monsters responsible for the crime and lock them away, that's a bonus.

Wimauma, just south of Tampa, is a rural town with a large migrant population amongst its 5,000 residents. We chose Wimauma for our outreach program. We set up our educational programs at two church missions located in the town. As in Immokalee, it didn't take long before our efforts started to pay off. And again it was a great way to get the migrant community familiar with our staff and for them to appreciate what we were all about and what we were trying to do.

After a slow first few months and lots of talking and listening on our part, the message we were desperate to convey started to make its mark. Pretty soon the migrants began to feel comfortable enough with us to report any potential trafficking scenarios to our office. They began calling us, day and night, if they had issues or needed assistance. Granted, many of the calls were to ask questions that had nothing to do human trafficking, but I didn't care. It showed they trusted us enough to reach out to our office. And it made me feel so proud that my staff and many of our volunteers had managed to guide these folks in the right direction and open up their minds in such a short period of time.

In the May of 2008, Gigi, now working as the event coordinator for the Clearwater office, and three of her volunteers went to Wimauma for one of our many sessions. They were all armed with bottles of water and information to give to the migrant workers. The bottles of water all had a special label that has information concerning human trafficking and phone numbers to call for assistance if they were suspicious of something going on. At this particular mission, the migrant workers received a bag full of groceries and a hot meal when they attended. The entire operation was run very well, and they accepted and encouraged what we were trying to do with open arms. During the meal, our group started handing out the bottles of water and chatted with the group.

The atmosphere in the hall was quite relaxed. The team sat and chatted with small groups or individuals dotted around the large hall while Gigi talked to the director of the mission about plans between our two organizations. Suddenly, three men burst through the main doors and into the hall. Everything stopped as all eyes turned to look at them.

The volunteers appeared at Gigi's side and nudged her. She looked across the room to the men standing near the doorway, looking nervously about. They were Mexican, around mid-thirties to forty years of age. They stood quite close to each other like they were afraid to be separated. One of the men looked about, the other two didn't make eye contact with anyone, and they stood there staring at their feet. They were all dressed in casual work clothes, jeans and T-shirts, very dirty and stained.

You could feel the tension in the room; the mood changed. Something didn't feel right. One of our volunteers approached the men and offered each a bottle of water. The men gladly accepted, but still they didn't move. They chugged the water down and sat there for a while. Then they left.

"Who are they?" Gigi whispered towards the director of the mission.

He shrugged his shoulders. "I don't know… I've never seen them before." They carried on handing out water and talking to the some of the other people at the mission.

A half-hour later, Brian, one of the volunteers, approached Gigi in a hurry.

"I think you better come, and I think you need to talk to them. I think it might be trafficking."

Immediately Gigi followed Brian into the other room and met up with the men sitting at a table by themselves, three empty plates in front of them.

"Hello," Gigi introduced herself to the men. She held out her hand, but they didn't shake it. They glared at her with suspicion. "Look we are not the police. We just want to talk with you and hopefully try and help you, but you need to be honest with us," she added.

Only one man looked up at her. He looked like he was a little older than the others. The two other men stood up to leave, until the older one, still sitting down, spoke up for the group. "Me and my friends are from Mexico." The other two men looked hesitant, but eventually they slumped back down next to him. "We were all smuggled into your country with a few other men across the border in California a few months ago… I don't know exactly where we ended up."

He gestured for her to join them. The rest of the canteen area was almost empty by now. She sat down. Gigi purposely let him carry on talking. But even as they talked, they still would not make eye contact with her.

He went on tell us how shortly after they had arrived in the United States, they met a man who said he could help them find a good paying job making $450 a week and they would get free room and board. He was also Mexican, and they all agreed since he seemed to be a really nice and genuine guy. He told them that he could get them a job picking vegetables in Florida and about all the money that they could send back home to their family.

"We believed him," the man said. The others nodded. "At first, everything was fine as we headed to Wimauma. During the trip down, we became friends with the man; he was really nice to us. He seemed helpful. We told him all about our families and where they lived. He asked us lots of questions about them. We know now that was a big mistake."

He gripped the water bottle in his hand so tightly he crushed it. "When we arrived, he took us all to a trailer in the forest on the edge of town."

"It was horrible," one of the other men spoke up, looking up at me for the first time. His face was drawn and weather-beaten, as if he'd been out in the sun too long.

The first man said there had been ten of them who had travelled with the man to Florida. The trailer he took them to was not only small, dirty, and cramped, there were already another eight men living there. They asked the man where they were going to sleep seeing there were already eight other men living there. The man told them it was not his problem.

"As soon as we entered the trailer," the man said, "we all owed him money for bringing us all to Florida. He told us not to worry because from the money we would earn, we would still be allowed to keep eight dollars from it."

"Why didn't you go?" the director asked him.

"The thing was," the man said, "he scared us because now we realized why he had asked us so many questions about our family. We had given this man information on our families and where they all lived. We thought he was a friend."

One of the men sitting by Gigi started to cry. He was an emotional wreck. The man told them that if they did not obey him, he would call his friend back in Mexico and have their families killed.

"He told me he would murder my little girl… twist her neck in two." The man in front of Gigi made the action with his hands. "He said he knew some powerful, nasty people and with just one phone call, someone would die."

Gigi couldn't believe how crafty and ruthless these traffickers were. While making small talk with these men, he was noting important things about them that he was going to use later on.

The man became really upset. No one said anything for a few minutes.

170

"What happened?" Gigi finally broke the ice. "How did you get here?"

"He locked us in the trailer that first night… all of us and he left us… no food… no way out of there," the first man spoke again.

He said the man had put a padlock on the trailer door, so there was no way to get out. Gigi physically shivered thinking what would have happened to these poor men if there had been a fire or another kind of emergency had happened where they had to get out.

"Couldn't you escape?" Gigi asked innocently.

"It was impossible… the other men had been there for six months. They told us they had tried and couldn't and said we should just listen to the man."

The next morning they were woken up just after sunrise and loaded up into a van. The man took all the men to the fields of Wimauma and put them to work. The first day they worked fourteen hours picking vegetables in the baking hot sun. In the middle of the day, they were given a little food, nothing much, and told to go back to work. At the end of the day, the man handed them all eight dollars in cash for their day's work but then took five dollars back for the food he had provided them to eat at lunchtime.

"For fourteen hours of work … we worked really hard … and we only received three dollars… three dollars… and then we were all taken back to the trailer and locked in… again with no food… nothing," one of the men muttered.

This went on weeks. Each day the man verbally abused them. He threatened them daily and, on a couple of occasions, he physically abused them as well.

"We were punched, slapped and kicked… but I could cope with that," the leader of the small group said. "The thing that scared me most was he was still making threats against my family. They were innocent in all of this."

One day the man locked the group in the trailer and informed them he was on his way to Mexico and while he was there he would be visiting their families, one by one. He smirked at each and every one of them.

"This freaked us all out… he was like the devil… pure evil. We tried to get out. It was torture," the leader explained. "While he was away, none of us knew what he was doing. We couldn't warn them… our family. Some nights I cried all night. I hate him. We've had enough."

When the man reappeared a day or so later, he laughed and told them that this time it was okay because he didn't have the time to make the visits.

"Even last night, he told us he's going back to Mexico in next few days and this time he was really going to harm one of our family's members," the second man spoke again.

"We couldn't take it anymore," the first man slammed the tabletop. "We decided that we had to do something in order to tell our families… to warn them. So once he took us to the fields this morning and left, we took off running and didn't stop until we reached this church." He looked at the door as if he was expecting it to open.

"'But he'll be searching for us," the third one finally spoke. "Once he knows we have gone… he'll do something to our families... I'm afraid… we all are." The others nodded.

"Okay, don't worry," Gigi's mind was running through what she needed to do. "We will take you away from here now and you can contact your family."

Gigi piled them into her car and drove them to a safe house about ten miles from the mission. Not ideal, but it would be all right for a short while. Some of the volunteers went shopping for food and clothes and other necessities that the men needed.

We got them a phone so they could call and tell their families what was going on. They seemed so happy to talk to their loved ones and have a shower and freshen themselves up. The next morning, Gigi talked to them about what we needed to do to stop this terrible man. Luckily, although they were illegal immigrants, it didn't take much convincing for the men to agree to come forward and speak to law enforcement.

Gigi called one of the Detectives from the Hillsborough County Sheriff's Office and advised him what had happened. He agreed to look into the allegations and set up a time to interview the men. After the first interview, Gigi received a call from the detective stating that this was "a textbook human trafficking case" and that they would start an investigation. The three men told us that seven other men had escaped with them, but they were in hiding.

The three men found the other seven and convinced them to also cooperate with the police, which they did. During this time my office provided services to the group of men. We gave them food and shelter and a little money for day-to-day things. Brian would accompany Gigi when she went to visit the group. He had really made a connection with them.

As June approached, the men became uneasy with their situation. They were in a new safe house, but because they didn't have a visa, they couldn't get any work. One of them told me that they needed to be able to work to send money to their families back home. "We need to move on," he said, "We are going to head north with the others. Their season is just beginning, and we've been told that there are plenty of jobs. We need to look after our families."

Gigi tried her best to convince the group to stay for the sake of their case. She tried to explain to them that without their input the case would fall apart. She wished we had the funds to really help them hang around until justice was done. But unfortunately, they were in desperate need for money, and they left in the middle of the night without telling us where they were headed.

The local police were trying to make a state case, but the prosecutors were taking too long. The police really cared about the case, but the workers just couldn't wait. The Mexican workers were worried that they were being set up to be deported. A lesson from this is that you can't string these people along with all kinds of promises. You have to do something for them to show your good faith.

When Gigi was told the sad news, she contacted the detective on the case to tell him.

"Let's try and get them back," he said.

"It's too late," Gigi replied.

They both knew it was no good. The case was suspended and the suspect released. Unfortunately, the men never did communicate back with our office, so the case was dropped.

Not for the first time, the man who had enslaved these men was never brought to justice and he's probably still out there somewhere involved with a different set of men. One thing I believe—his time will come!

Around the same time the men from the trailer were leaving, Gigi received a phone call from another man, Mr. Lee. Over the phone, he sounded very anxious and told her that he had been advised to contact our office by Catholic Charities.

"I recently married a woman," he mentioned. "I worked at a Thai Restaurant. She's from Thailand. Jane is her name. She is so nice. Can you help us?"

Gigi thought he was phoning from a pay phone on a busy street. There was a lot of traffic noise in the background, and it was quite hard to hear what he was saying as he talked.

"So why are you phoning us?" Gigi tried to make sense of their conversation from the snippets.

"The owners of the restaurant still have her passport. They will not give it back. The church told me to call you... to tell you....Can you do anything... please?"

"What?" Gigi said, still not fully understanding what he wanted from us.

"They said that my wife may be a victim of human trafficking."

Gigi jumped into action like a soldier on the front line. Gigi scheduled an appointment to meet with him and his new bride, Jane, as soon as possible. Three days later they met up at Gigi's office. As soon as they walked in, Gigi could tell they were in love. They were such a perfect couple together. She was fifty-seven years old, quiet, shy and very pretty. He was a few year's younger, an American, small in size but thickset and extremely pleasant. They held hands the entire time we were together.

During the assessment, Gigi learned Jane had recently arrived from Thailand on a tourist visa. Back in Thailand, she worked as a caretaker for an elderly woman for a couple of years. The elderly woman's only daughter had married an American and had left Thailand to live in Florida. There, the daughter and her husband opened up a Thai restaurant and were very successful.

A year before Jane arrived in the States, the elderly woman whom she took care of became seriously ill and, after suffering for a few short weeks, died. Jane cried as she told me how lovely the woman had been to work for and how kind she had been to her and her own family. After the mother's death, the daughter called up from America to thank Jane for everything that she had done for her mother when she was alive and for the family since her death. Then out of the blue, the daughter said she wanted to show her appreciation by bringing Jane to Florida for a vacation. "My mother would have wanted me to do this for you," she said.

"I said no at first," Jane said, "I was scared to go. I'd never been out of Thailand, and I'd heard America was not a very nice place to go to."

But she said the daughter called several times and, after some coaxing, Jane finally gave in and said she would go.

"The daughter helped me apply for a tourist visa and bought me a one-way ticket from Thailand to Florida."

Gigi looked up at her. "They only brought you a one-way ticket?"

Jane knew where that question was leading. "I did ask her why it was only a one-way ticket," she seemed embarrassed, "But she told me that it would be cheaper to buy her a ticket back home separately when I got there… I believed her."

As soon as Jane arrived at the Tampa International Airport, she was greeted by the daughter and her American husband. Both were extremely nice to her and took her on a brief tour of the area in their "open-top car."

"It was so beautiful," she told me. "So nice… not what I had expected… and not what I had heard it was like. I felt so happy," she added.

This reminded Gigi of Alicia's story. She guessed what was coming next.

Jane continued, "After our drive, they took me to the restaurant which they owned. We had a meal… it was wonderful."

Then when the restaurant closed and everyone left including the staff, they dropped the bombshell. They stood above her as she sat in her chair and told her in no uncertain terms that the cost of the airline ticket to bring her here had been really expensive and now she owed them lots of money for bringing her over to America.

"I was shocked," she said, "I didn't have money… only enough money for my visit and some money to buy my family some presents from America. I told them this. They didn't listen. They were very serious." She stopped talking.

"It's okay," Gigi tried to comfort her. "Jane, don't get upset. Take your time."

She smiled. "I didn't know what to do. They had been so nice to me." She gripped her husband's hand tightly. "The woman said that I could work in her restaurant to help pay the money I owed them and then maybe I could get a ticket to go home."

Gigi could see by her husband's face that he was getting angry.

"I didn't know what to do. I didn't know anyone else, so I couldn't ask for help. I didn't speak the language. I was so scared… so afraid… so I said yes to them." She glanced at him as if it was her fault. "What was I supposed to do?"

To make matters worse, later that night, the couple took away her visa, her passport and all of her personal belongings. She was only allowed to keep her clothing. They marched her to a small room at the back of the kitchen of the restaurant. In the room were a small bed, a TV, and a set of drawers where she could store her clothing.

"This is where you will live," the woman barked at her. They both left, leaving her sitting there in the dark, alone and confused.

The next morning the husband turned up and told Jane she would be the new cook. She started her day off at seven in the morning, prepping the food for the day. She would work non-stop until midnight, doing whatever she was told to do. She was not given a key to the restaurant. This meant she couldn't leave because she would be locked out and have nowhere to go.

Of course whatever money Jane earned went back to the couple to pay off her debt. With no money, she lived on the scraps of food from the kitchen.

"A couple of months later," Mr. Lee spoke up, "I began to work at the restaurant as a dish washer. Straight away I noticed Jane. I thought she was lovely, but she didn't speak English and I did not speak Thai, so we didn't talk at first. But I could see the owners treated her much differently from the rest of the staff. They were unkind to her—always shouting and yelling at her."

However, he said, over time they became friends. "I felt sorry for her. I wanted to help her." He began to learn to speak Thai and she began to understand English more, so they started to communicate with each other. He said he could tell that Jane was tired and afraid.

Soon after Mr. Lee and Jane became friends, he asked her out to dinner. She said no at first, but he kept asking until she agreed, but she told him not to tell the owners or she would get in trouble. On their night out, he learned Jane was not allowed to leave the restaurant and that she actually lived in the kitchen. Little by little, Mr. Lee started putting the pieces together of what had been happening to her. Several months later, he decided he wanted to help Jane. After the restaurant closed one night, he came back and helped her to pack her clothes. She was afraid and didn't want to go at first. But he finally persuaded her everything would be all right, and he helped her escape. Of course in the morning when the couple opened the restaurant and found she was gone, they began to contact all of the workers until they found that Jane was with Mr. Lee.

"They showed up at my door, shouting and screaming and demanded that Jane be returned to them," he explained. "I called the police, but when they came, all they did was ask the couple to leave the premises and they went away."

Mr. Lee and Jane then went to Catholic Charities in hope that they could change Jane's visa status and assist in obtaining her passport. After they finished telling their story and Gigi completed the assessment, she set about contacting law enforcement. We provided Jane with services to assist her in settling in her new life. Law enforcement investigated the case and was able to obtain Jane's passport, but nothing happened to the couple. They said that they didn't have enough evidence, and the case was closed.

Mr. Lee and Jane are still very much in love and living together. The happy couple still pop in to see us every now and again. They seem so grateful for all the help and support we gave them to set up their new life together. But not all the victims we have helped have been appreciative. I had a survivor once, a woman we rescued from a lifetime of prostitution, tell me that she thought because she had been exploited in the United States that we owed her for the rest of her life. I don't think she realized how much hard work and time it took to keep all our victims happy and keep my staff from being worn out. Thankfully most victims and their families appreciate the work we do for them and even help us with new victims.

Human trafficking doesn't just begin on foreign soil. My team and I got involved in a case where we were asked to help find a girl from Alabama whose family believed was a victim in labor trafficking. Eighteen-year-old Danielle was reported missing by her mother after responding to a "Help Wanted" advertisement placed in a magazine by a door-to-door sales business.

The advertisement was for a full-time position that included "a good rate of pay and exciting travel opportunities." The rest of the advertisement appeared pretty vague but attractive enough for Danielle to give the number a call. During the call, she was put through to a guy named Tom. He sounded enthusiastic about the prospects the job had to offer. After a short phone interview consisting of questions about her and her experience, she was hired and told to come to Miami to begin work as soon as she could. In the first week of January, her mother took her to catch the morning Greyhound bus from Mobile, Alabama. Her mother later told me she didn't like her going. She felt something wasn't right. "I told her not to go, but she insisted. She told me not to worry."

Mother and daughter hugged each other and said their goodbyes. They waved to each other as the bus disappeared out of sight. A few hours later, Danielle's mother received a call from Danielle to say she had arrived safely in Miami and had been picked up by a representative from the company. She said she was on her way to Fort Lauderdale, Florida, and everything was fine. That was the last time Danielle used her own cell phone to call home.

Danielle's mother tried her several times on her cell, but it went straight through to voice mail.

"I became concerned over my daughter's safety when I couldn't contact her, and then I received a call from her a week later, but this time from a pay phone," Danielle's mother recounts.

During the brief and awkward conversation, Danielle said she was doing great, but then she strangely ended their chat by telling her mother she had to go because she wasn't supposed to be calling.

"What do you mean you're not supposed to be calling?" her mother asked. "Why? What's going on?"

But her daughter had already hung up by this point. Danielle was gone.

Frantically the mother attempted to call several of the phone numbers listed for the company. Most of her calls were not answered. The calls which someone did pick up she found she was speaking with a company representatives who told her quite abruptly she was not allowed to speak to her own daughter. Often the phone would go dead halfway through the conversation.

After several days of failed attempts to contact Danielle, her mother filed a missing person's report, and the teenager was entered into the Alabama Crime Information Center as missing. In mid-January, at the mother's request, an officer of the Mobile County Sheriff's Office made several phone calls to try to contact someone from the company who had placed the advertisement.

The police officer finally reached a female representative who called herself Sally. When asked about the whereabouts of Danielle and why she had not contacted her mother, Sally told the officer that she didn't understand the point of concern because Danielle was an adult and that she could not give an address for her because she was "traveling all over the place" doing her job as a door-to-door sales rep.

Our office got involved in February as Danielle still hadn't called home although she had been spotted in Tampa. My team and I were basically there as a support system for the family and to spread the word about the missing girl through all of our contacts. Whenever Danielle was spotted, we would contact law enforcement in that particular town or city where she had been seen to see if they could try and locate her. We got many calls about Danielle; some proved helpful and accurate, however many did not.

One day in early March, one of my team members got the chance to speak to Danielle for a couple of minutes when she called her family and they connected our office up on three-way call.

It was quite obvious from the brief conversation something wasn't right. We had never spoken to her before, but the team member could tell Danielle was lying to her. She sounded nervous, and it sounded as if she had a script in front of her that she was following. Our staff tried to test her by asking her questions she didn't expect. It worked because she did not know how to answer some of them.

By her hesitation, we assumed she was either giving herself time to think of her answer or she was checking with someone first before replying. One of the basic questions we asked was what she did for her birthday, which was earlier that same week.

"Oh," she finally answered rather unconvincingly, "I had lots of fun with my friends… We ate a lot of pizza."

"Did you do anything else to celebrate?" we pushed again.

Silence.

"Danielle… did you go anywhere else?"

"Ummmm… I went fishing as well," she finally blurted out, "'It was great fun… fishing was fun."

"Oh fishing… that sounds good… what did you catch?"

Again she hesitated. The team member repeated the question.

"I'm not sure," she added. And them the phone went dead.

We agreed with her mother's gut feeling that there was something going on with Danielle. Over the next several months, she was located twice by police during the course of traffic stops, once in Florida and once in Lynchburg, Virginia. Each time her ID was run and the officers saw she was reported as missing. Yet when they questioned her about this, she informed them that she was fine, and that she was an adult and had no wish to return home.

She made it sound like she was happy with what she was doing. Each time the police let her go. And what's more, due to her identifications at these stops, Danielle was removed from the missing persons list.

When the family found out, they demanded she be re-entered onto the list. After speaking to some of the officers who had talked to her and also after investigating the company she was supposed to be working for, they suspected she was being transported around the country and made to sell magazine subscriptions door-to-door against her will. The big question was why and why did she tell the police she was all right?

This was not the first time there had been complaints about young people forced to work for these types of companies. Reports had been circulated through the nationwide Better Business Bureau about the tactics used by such door-to-door subscription businesses. We saw emails from the family to the authorities suggesting their daughter's situation fell under the category of labor trafficking, although there was no official evidence to support the claim.

With the search increasing, Danielle was located by law enforcement a third time in July when the vehicle she was in was again stopped for a traffic violation. This time Danielle's older sister was called during the stop. Danielle was taken to one side and allowed to speak to her sister. It was a long emotional conversation, after which Danielle informed the police officer she wanted to go home. She was promptly taken to the Dallas airport and flown to Mobile, where she was picked up by family.

Even today Danielle's circumstances during that time remain unclear. She refused to open up about what happened to her when she was with the company. She became nervous and anxious whenever asked why she didn't leave. All she was willing to say was she was really happy to be back home and she felt as if a huge weight had been lifted off her shoulders.

Not surprisingly, law enforcement has yet to investigate or prosecute the company after several of the police officials who had picked her up made statements that she told them she was in good health and did not wish to return home.

This was disappointing because I believe the company and its methods should have been investigated. At least Danielle is now home. Her mother sent everyone involved in helping to get her daughter back a heart-felt message thanking us all for our assistance in finding her. It ended by saying Danielle was doing well, was very happy to be home, and was spending much-needed, quality time with family members. After that, the family refused to talk to anyone about what went on and went back to trying to lead normal lives.

To be honest I don't really blame them; they had been through enough worry and stress, but some members of the media were skeptical. Some didn't believe Danielle was a victim at all because she didn't come out and tell her story. It is sad that some people only believe that we have trafficking victims if a victim comes forward and agrees to be interviewed by the media or speak out about their experiences in public. Maybe they don't realize that under the Trafficking Victims Protection Act, the victims have the right to privacy and confidentiality and not everyone wants to relive what they had gone through. And believe me, besides Danielle, our office received phone calls on four other young adults who had experienced they exact thing that Danielle had just gone through.

Call to Action

In 1865, the United States outlawed slavery with the Thirteenth Amendment to the United States Constitution. Section One of the amendment stated that *"neither slavery nor involuntary servitude, except as a punishment for crime whereof the party shall have been duly convicted, shall exist within the United States, or any place subject to their jurisdiction."*

Brave words, indeed, for the time. Yet it took over a century of suffering, anguish and bloodshed until people really started to believe that slavery in the country had finally been abolished. I, like many, thought those dark days were truly behind us—until I rescued Chica. Now I know that slavery is bigger and more sinister than ever and exists in all walks of our society.

There is still so much work to be done, so many people to educate about the effects of human trafficking throughout the world. In the end, it's all about saving the victims. We must all fight to improve their right to live a normal decent life.

People go to jail if they treat an animal badly. Yet it seems much easier to get away with mistreating a human being. It doesn't make sense. Consider how many animal shelters there are in most cities. Compare that to the number of places for human trafficking victims to get help. It angers me that there are no places to house victims, no places for them to sleep, no experts to care for them. We treat animals better than we treat human beings.

The fight against the traffickers is not easy. They always seem to be one step ahead of the authorities. They are clever as well as ruthless. But that's what greed does to people.

Rescuing the victims and helping them back into society is a bit like finding a sick bird with a wing broken. I need to keep them safe, give them love and care until they are ready to fly again. It's not easy—many of the victims are traumatized. One girl couldn't see a police office without feeling like committing suicide. It took years for mental scars to heal.

Yet, things are changing for the better. Like the T1 visa law which came because of victims like Chica, laws are being established to fight this ever-growing crime in governments the world over.

At the Palermo Convention in 2000, the United Nations adopted the Protocol to Prevent, Suppress and Punish Trafficking in Persons, especially Women and Children." Since the protocol was adopted, 146 nations have ratified it and 128 have enacted comprehensive anti-trafficking laws. This is a giant step forward. This is real progress.

Victim protection is arguably even more important than holding traffickers accountable. Yet the number of victims identified worldwide dropped thirty-two percent from 49,105 in 2009 to 33,113 in 2010. Despite the awareness-raising report, US- and UN-sponsored training, and a yearlong CNN campaign, trafficking victims are still being doubly victimized when treated by society and law enforcement as dirty, disposable, and deportable.

Our role at FCAHT has always been to ensure the victims are given every chance to start a new life after all the trauma. In my relatively short time involved in the fight against human trafficking my team, and I have tried many things to ensure the victims adapt to some kind of normal way of life as quickly as possible.

As part of our program at FCAHT, we developed an art therapy program in 2007. We wanted get all the victims to be a part of a larger family-like group and not to feel that they were the only ones that had gone through such suffering and pain. We also wanted to provide them with an outlet where they could express themselves and maybe put down on paper how they were feeling or what they had been through or simply what they wanted their world to be like.

Local businesses donated material, paint and brushes and students from the University of Florida and community volunteers facilitated the program. We tried to make it into a fun event for all of the victims, and all of us. We didn't lay down any rules or guidelines, just gave them the materials and let them go for it.

It was moving to see the victim's story told through their artwork. Many of the paintings they created were so powerful, they took my breath away. Just by looking at them I could feel the emotion, the sadness, the energy right there on the canvas. I couldn't believe how artistic some of our survivors were. One of our survivors was expecting a baby, and she painted a fetus captioned "Give me a chance to live". It gave me goose bumps. I've seen people standing, staring at it with tears running down their faces.

We have all of the paintings displayed around our office, and any time someone wants to meet a victim, we invite them to come there to meet the victims through their work. It's great to see the victim explain and talk about their life through their art they have created.

We took the paintings around the state to be exhibit at Florida Gulf Coast University, Rollins College, Sanibel Resort, Fort Myers Historical Museum and other locations throughout the region. The free exhibits expanded our human trafficking awareness and education campaign. Interested people flocked to every event, and the feedback was wonderful.

People have often asked about buying the paintings, and though flattered by the offers, I have refused to sell them. In a way, that would be profiting off the suffering of others. Also the paintings are part of our life and work. I cherish seeing them every day, and they remind me daily that, like the survivors who created the art, there are many others waiting to be rescued. Looking at the paintings when I walk into the office every morning helps me to carry on with my crusade even when I'm at my lowest.

I have heard that some other agencies sell the artwork or jewelry made by the human trafficking victims in their care to make a profit for their own organizations. I would rather struggle than use the victim's work to make money for my agency. I feel that by doing that I would be repeating what the traffickers were doing to them—exploiting them for money.

I know we need funding to survive, but I don't believe survivors should have to make the jewelry or any merchandise to be sold by the same agency that is providing them with the services. I don't believe it is right and ethical. I hope and pray that those organizations reconsider their policy and stop using the suffering of others to make money for themselves.

It is also sad that as more people get involved in the fight against human trafficking, more in-fighting is stirred up. It's terrible to see all the territorial wars between state, local and federal law enforcement as well as the non-governmental agencies and faith-based groups that have organized human trafficking organizations. The constant attacks, lies and false accusations have taken a toll on many of the genuine people who are compassionate and have a passion for the cases.

We must stop attacking each other and learn to work together. In the competition for limited funding, we have forgotten that we are supposed to identify, rescue and restore victims of human trafficking. This is not about fame or money. It is about human beings.

In the struggle for human rights, there is still plenty of room for improvement. It is sad, but it is the truth that human trafficking has become a political tool. It is all about "who you know" and who likes you. Human trafficking has become an issue of money and high payroll checks for the administrative positions. I have heard of executive directors making $90,000.00 to $160,000.00 a year running non-profit organizations, leaving only a small amount of funding available for the program and services to the victims.

This is wrong. There should be a cap for salaries for individuals running these non-profit organizations. This would make sure the majority of the funds are used and spent in the right places—victim services, outreach and community awareness. I have seen how agencies embellish the numbers of "victims" they are helping and the programs they are involved in just to look good when they submit their grants report. I have seen how good agencies and passionate people have left the field because of the territorial wars.

When I started working in human trafficking cases, no one cared about the crime until July 16, 2004, when President George W. Bush came to Tampa, Florida, to speak at the first National Human Trafficking Conference. During his speech he stated that he was allocating federal funding to fight human trafficking in the United States. The phrase that pays—*federal dollars*. After the funding was released, the grassroots agency that were working human trafficking cases prior to that conference had to compete for funding with new organizations that lacked experience and knowledge of human trafficking but saw dollar signs. We then started seeing more self-proclaimed "experts" in the field. Suddenly the focus became competition for the almighty dollar, rather than helping the victims.

We have to understand that human trafficking is happening right here in the United States. We also need financial resources to help and provide services to the victims we rescue, right here in the United States. We need to build short-term and long-term shelters for the victims. We need to feed them, clothe them and provide them with the care and affection they deserve as human beings. We need to give back to them their rights not take them away like the traffickers and pimps do.

We have to give them back their dignity, including the right to choose—not force our beliefs like the Christian group that would not allow victims to have birth control pills. We have to give them the right to make decisions for themselves—or else we are treating them just like the pimps and traffickers.

We need to have more financial support from the government and the private sector. We need to understand that victims are found right here and need services. We need to understand that today, our own citizens are also vulnerable of being trafficked for sex and labor. We need to understand that "reverse trafficking" is happening in the United States. In the same way people are being trafficked into the United States, American citizens are being recruited and trafficked outside the United States.

The only way we are going to make a difference in the fight against human trafficking is if we all come together and fight this evil together. What if the readers of this book bonded together to become twenty-first century abolitionists? The actions of one person can make a difference—just like Alicia's church friends or Conchita's high school friend Pablo or Father Ray and his wife, Ning, or Maria's neighbor, Yoanna, or Josephine's boyfriend Mr. Lee. The actions of one can save the life of another.

The last thirteen years or so have been a rollercoaster ride for me and my family and everyone else involved in FCHAT. I've seen things I'd never imagined went on in this world. I've been lucky to meet some of the nicest people anyone would like to meet, but I've also set eyes on pure evil. I've reached the lowest of lows during that time, but when rescuing these children and knowing they are safe, I've reached up to the highest points anyone can ever reach.

As of me, I am blessed with a wonderful family. I am still fighting against human trafficking and I will survive no matter what I come up against. It's been a little over two years since I've collected a salary, but I am committed to continuing the fight to save more lives. That is my mission, and it will continue until God sends me another.

I have dreams. In the United States, we do not have enough shelters dedicated to victims of human trafficking, male and female. I dream of a day when "Harriet House" will be open, providing shelter to victims of human trafficking not only in Florida but all over the United States. Harriet House, in honor of one of my heroes, Harriet Tubman, would be a place survivors can call home. A place they'll receive one-on-one counseling. A place where they can be empowered to transition into new lives. A place where the survivors can follow the "north star" and see freedom on the horizon. That is my dream.

But the most important dream I have is that we can eradicate slavery and live in peace and freedom. We must unite and stop the attacks and territorial wars among non-governmental organizations, law enforcement, and faith-based agencies. We must keep human trafficking away from politics. These are human beings who deserve to be identified, rescued, restored, protected and freed from slavery. We must UNITE and work together to make sure we all can live in peace and free of slavery around the world. I would like to thank God for giving me the strength to keep fighting for freedom. God bless all of you, and please, let's make the world a better place to live without wars and slavery.

There is a painting in the coalition office showing some chains with a dark background. The links are being broken in the middle. The chains glow in the dark. My husband suggested I write a book to shine some light into the darkness that is human trafficking.

I pray that these words glow.

APPENDIX

Human trafficking can only continue and grow if the victims remain invisible in the eyes and the mind of the general public. I believe my role has changed significantly over the years—from finding and rescuing the victims, to now removing the veil of ignorance that surrounds the subject.

For the slave trade to cease to exist, or at least to decrease, it will take an organized and sustained effort from everyone. Our actions must be community-wide, countrywide, and even worldwide for change to take place. It all starts with engaging the community so they can serve as intermediaries in detecting human trafficking in their area and to ensure the right services are available with the right groups to care for the victims.

The more people who know what to look for as far as the indicators are concerned the better. It starts with understanding where the hot spots are and where human trafficking regularly takes place. It can differ from region to region, but the list below is just a sample of the most common hot spots.

- Working in agricultural roles like picking fruit
- Housecleaning services
- Domestic servants
- Nail salons
- Hotels
- Casinos
- Landscape and gardening industries
- Construction sites
- Garment factories
- Red light districts
- Strip clubs
- Massage parlors
- Magazine Sales Crew
- Ethnic Food Restaurants
- Private Country Clubs

This list is by no means complete because as we have seen in this book, slavery can exist in all walks of life. The trick is to get people to look at the world around them with a new set of eyes, and maybe ask a different set of questions.

Body language is very important. When dealing with a potential victim, you will notice that they do not make eye contact with you. The potential victim will basically look like an emotionless robot. They do not laugh. They seem anxious or depressed. They just don't smile. They appear to be worn out. You can see bags under their eyes. Many of these victims will show signs of malnourishment. Some of the victims may also have signs of physical abuse. They may not identify themselves as victims. They may not speak English. Likely to lie or use rehearsed stories initially, they may be behaviorally dependent on trafficker. Their cultural or religious backgrounds may deter victims from telling the full story. Victims may be reluctant to speak to anyone wearing a gun, badge, or uniform because they are conditioned to fear law enforcement.

In some situations, you may notice that the conversations with the potential victims are very hurried. If you continue trying to push a conversation, you may notice that that worker may end up getting in trouble. Some of the traffickers will tell their victims what to say and what not to say. You can tell that their conversations are scripted.

At times, you may notice that outside of the business, you may find a large conversion van. If you see the servers and cooks leaving for the night in a van, they may be trafficking victims. If you see that the workers do not go out on their own, it can be a red flag. If you get a chance to see where the vans go, you will see that all of the workers live in the same apartment/house. Things that people can notice in their own neighbourhoods is large amounts of men and women living in a home. Especially if they notice that at the end of the day all of the people in the home arrive from work together or a large number of residents getting into the van together early in the morning.

With sex trafficking some of the indicators can be different:

- Excess amount of cash---One thing you can look for is if a child who is homeless or comes from an impoverished background who has new clothes, shoes, cell phones, anything expensive and you know that there is no way this child can afford these expensive items.
- Hotel room keys
- Chronic runaway/homeless youth
- Signs of branding (tattoo, jewelry)
- Lying about age/false identification
- Inconsistencies in story
- Lack of knowledge of a given community or whereabouts
- Presence of an overly controlling and abusive "boyfriend"
- Inability or fear to make eye contact
- Injuries/signs of physical abuse or torture
- Restricted/scripted communication
- Demeanor – fear, anxiety, depression, submissive, tense, nervous

Some of the questions we ask when face with a potential victims:

Immigration:

- What is their immigration status?
- How did they enter the U.S.?
- Do they have personal documents, such as identification papers, passports, birth certificates?
- Who is in control of documents and travel arrangements?
- Do they have authorization to work in the U.S.?
- Were they told what to say to immigration agents or officials when they arrived?

Employment:

- Did they come to the U.S. for a specific job or purpose?
- Are they doing different work than expected?
- Who is their employer?
- Does their employer provide housing, food, clothes, or uniforms?
- Employment contract: What did it say?
- Do they owe money to their employer?
- Did employer/boss tell them what to say to police?
- Were they forced to have sex as part of the job?
- Can they freely leave employment/ situation?
- What happened if they make a mistake at work?
- Does the employer hold wages?
- Are there guards at work or video cameras to monitor and make sure no one leaves?

Safety/Coercion:

- Have victims been threatened with harm if they try to leave?
- What is their understanding of what would happen if they left the job?
- What would happen if they went home or were returned to their home country?
- Have they been threatened with reporting to immigration or deportation?
- Have they been physically harmed: deprived of food, water, sleep, medical care, or other life necessities?
- Had anyone threatened their family?
- Were they kidnapped or sold?

Social Networks:

- Are they allowed to buy clothes and food on their own?
- Can they come and go as they please?
  Are there rules about this?

- Can they freely contact (phone, write) friends and family?
- Are they free to have a relationship with someone?
- Are they isolated from the community
- Can they bring friends home?
- Are minors allowed to attend school?

If you suspect human trafficking is taking place or suspect you know someone suffering at the hands of slavery, please contact any agency in your area or call us.

P. O. Box 2948
Clearwater, FL 33775-2948

Phone: (727) 442-3064
Fax: (727) 442-3531

stophumantrafficking.org
24-Hour National Human Trafficking Hotline: (888) 373-7888

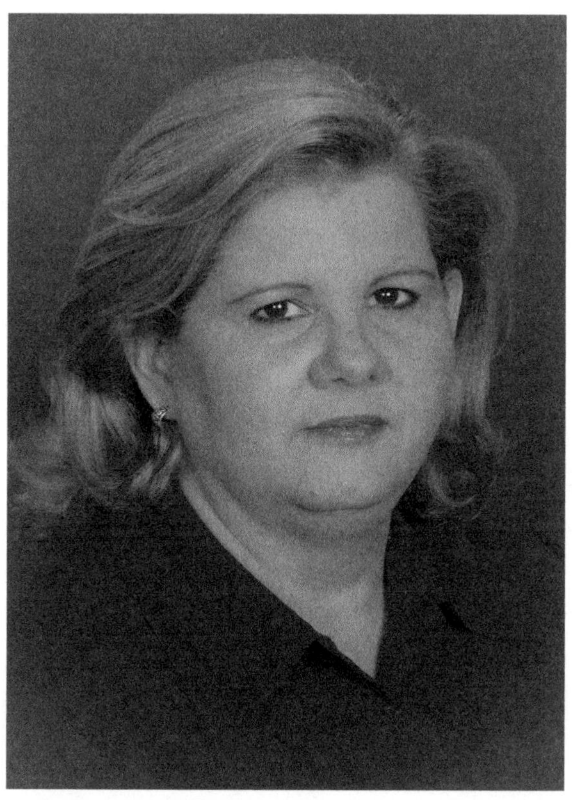

Anna Rodriguez is the founder and executive director of Florida Coalition Against Human Trafficking (FCAHT). She has been recognized for her work from leaders around the world including Former President George W. Bush, Senator John Ashcroft, Diputada Stella Cordoba, etc. She has been featured on CBS Evening News, CBS Early Show, Fox News, CNN etc. She has also been featured in news articles in the Miami Times, New York Post, Atlanta Journal etc. She has been instrumental in leading books and movies on human trafficking including David Batstones' book NOT FOR SALE, a documentary produced by Robert Macarrelli, Lives for Sale by Maryknoll, Slavery in Florida and Cargo Innocence Lost by Michael Corey Davis. Anna travels the world (Guatemala, Argentina, Puerto Rico, Peru, Chile, Dominican Republic, Bolivia, Uruguay, Jamaica, Costa Rica, London, Belize, Dominica, San Salvador, Ecuador etc.) speaking and training law enforcement agencies, immigration and government officials, community organizations and faith based organizations on human trafficking.

In 2011 Anna was inducted into Florida Women's Hall of Fame. Most recently she was awarded the prestigious MAKERS award and was named Vice President for RATT Mercosur, which is an International Coalition of Anti Human Trafficking groups around the world.

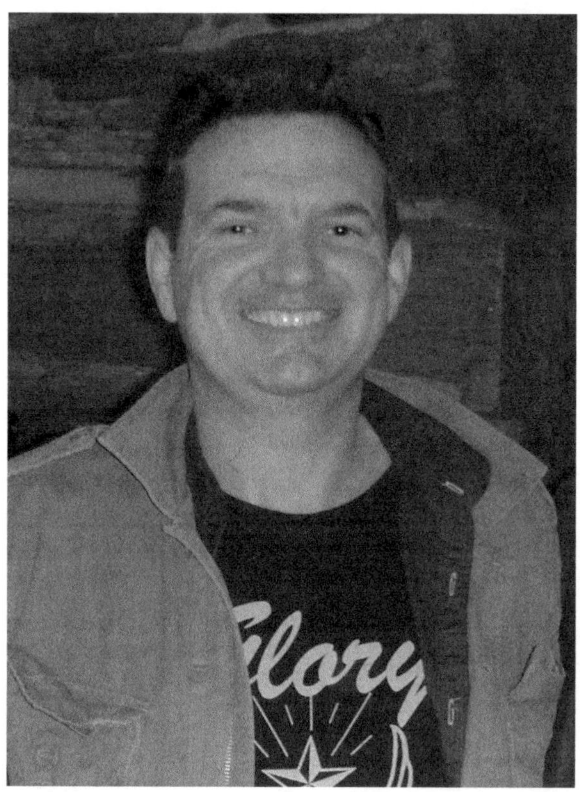

Anthony Bunko began writing a decade ago. During that time he's had several fiction and non-fiction novels published, most notably, the highly acclaimed comedy novel, The Tale of the Shagging Monkeys, an award-winning book on visual poetry and the autobiography of the late, great Stuart Cable, drummer with the UK rock band, the Stereophonics.

He resides in Merthyr Tydfil in Wales in the United Kingdom and works as a self-employed business consultant but devotes himself to writing in all forms.

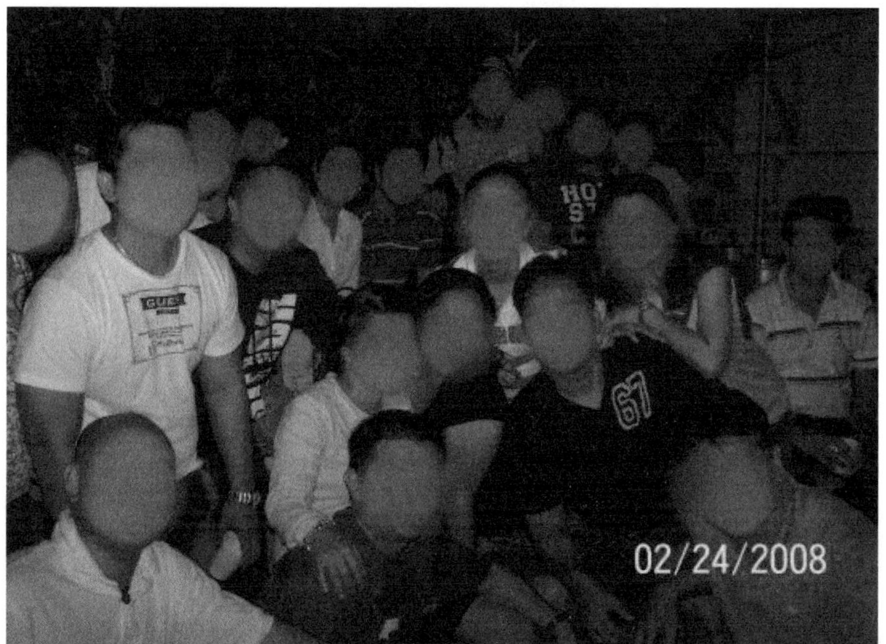

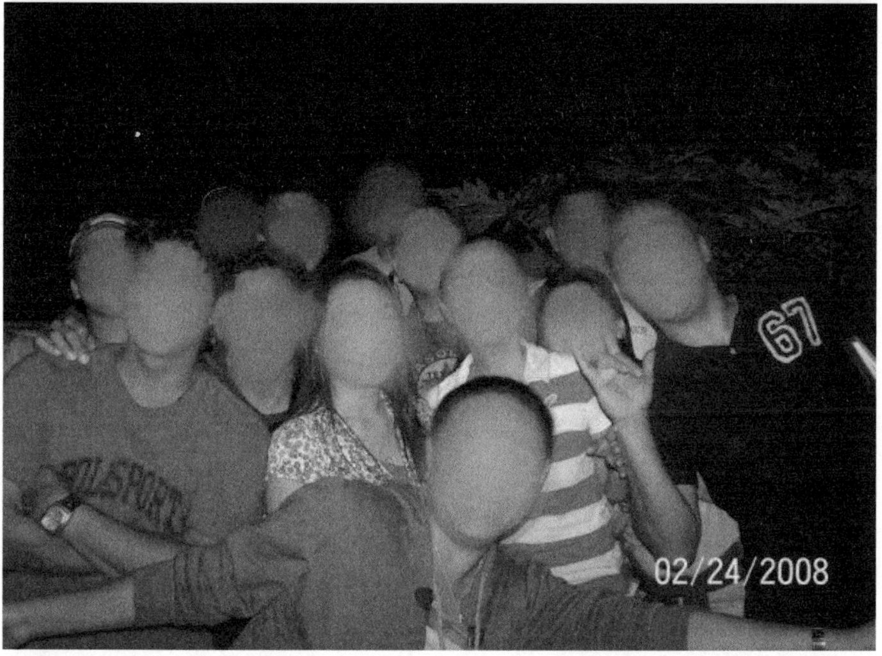

2008: LABOR TRAFFICKING CASE known as the BOCA39 case.

2010: Traffickers plead guilty and are now serving time in fedral prison. Survivors now have been re-unified with family and are living in freedom.

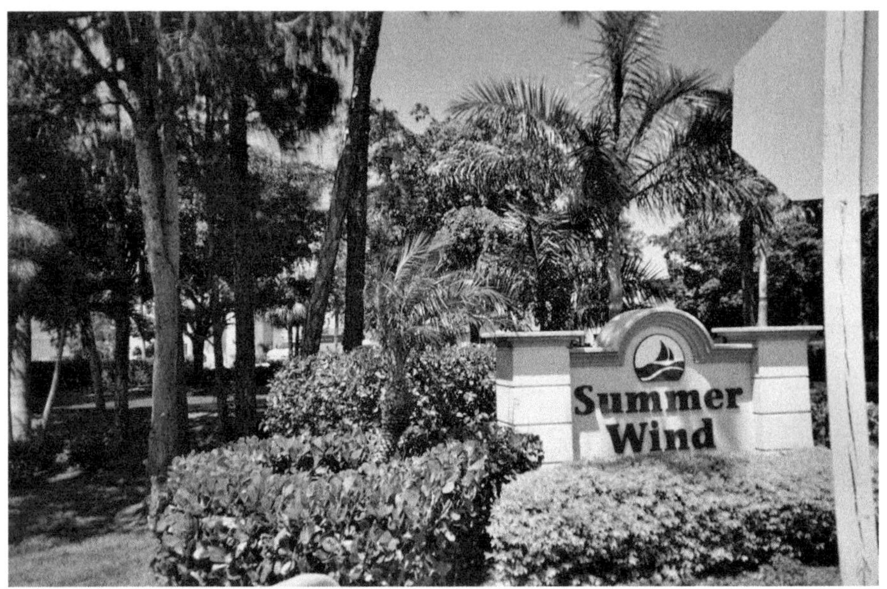

Summer Wind Apartments.
Alicia was found and rescued.

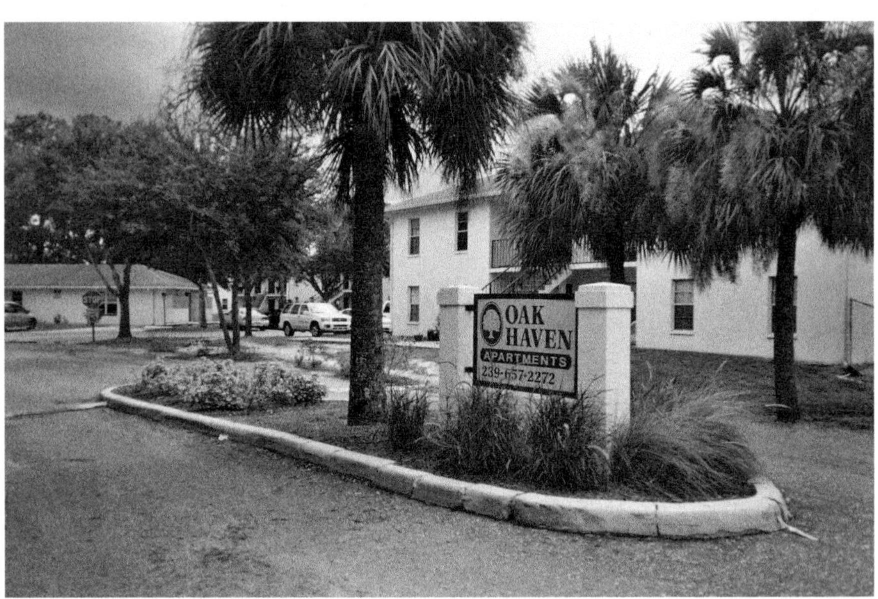

Oak Haven Apartments.
Tecum Case.
Chica was found and rescued.

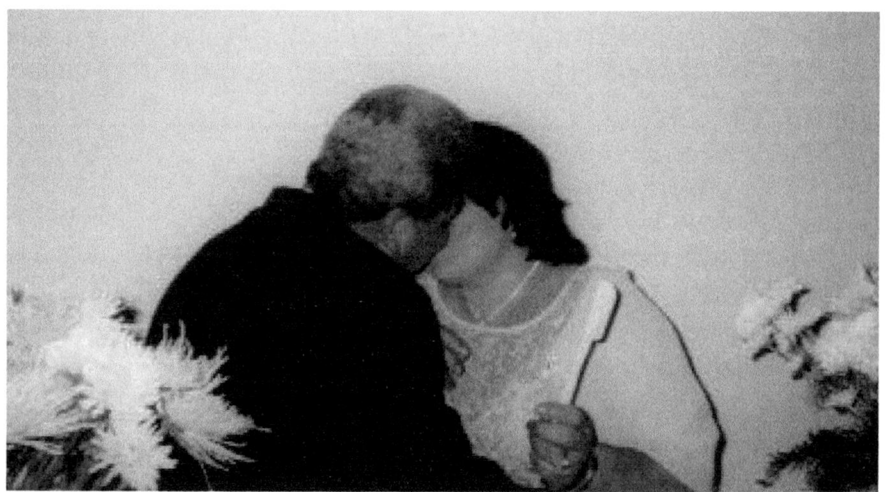

Alicia's Wedding- Husband and wife's first kiss.
Ceremony officiated by Anna Rodriguez, Notary Public.

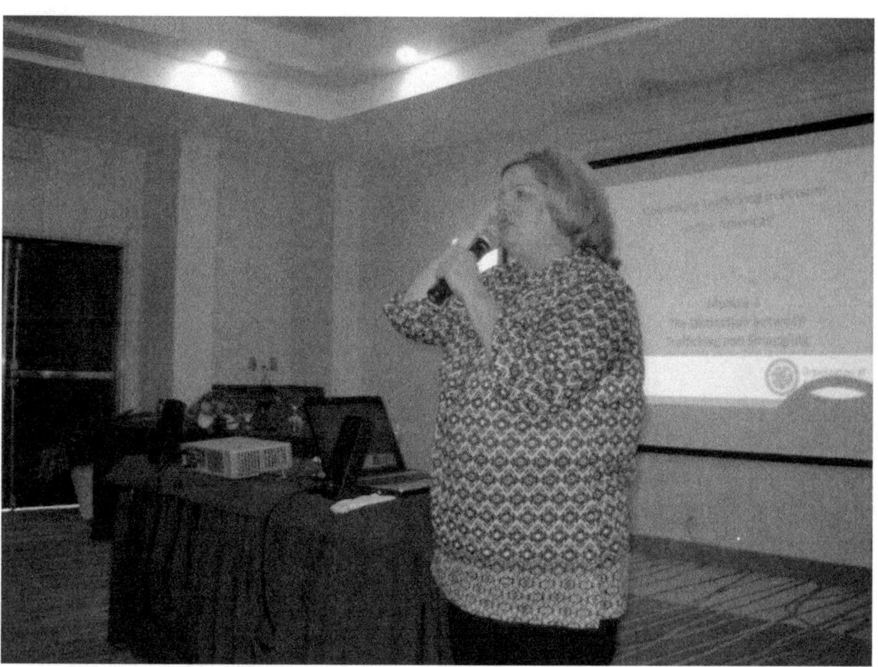

Anna Rodriguez Training Law Enforcement in St. Lucia.

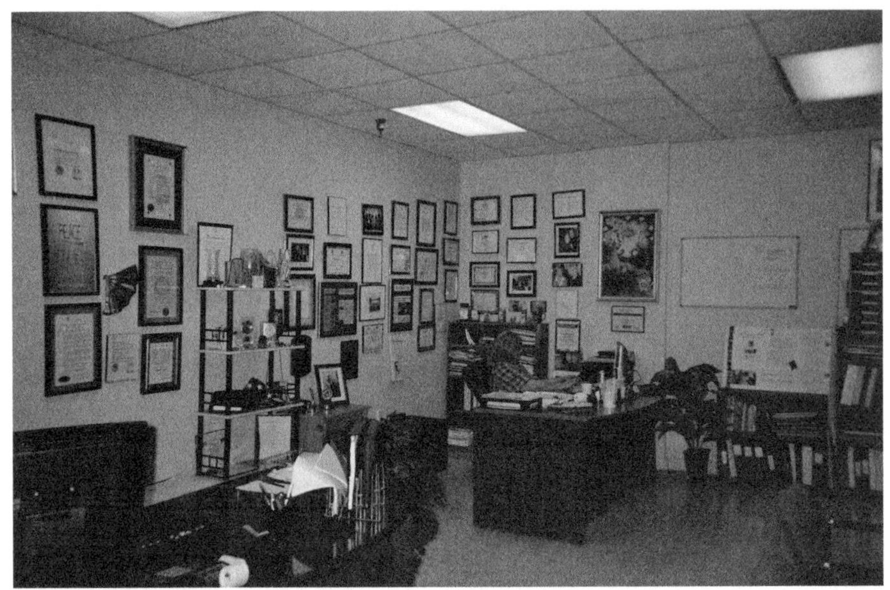

Anna Rodriguez awards and recognitions.

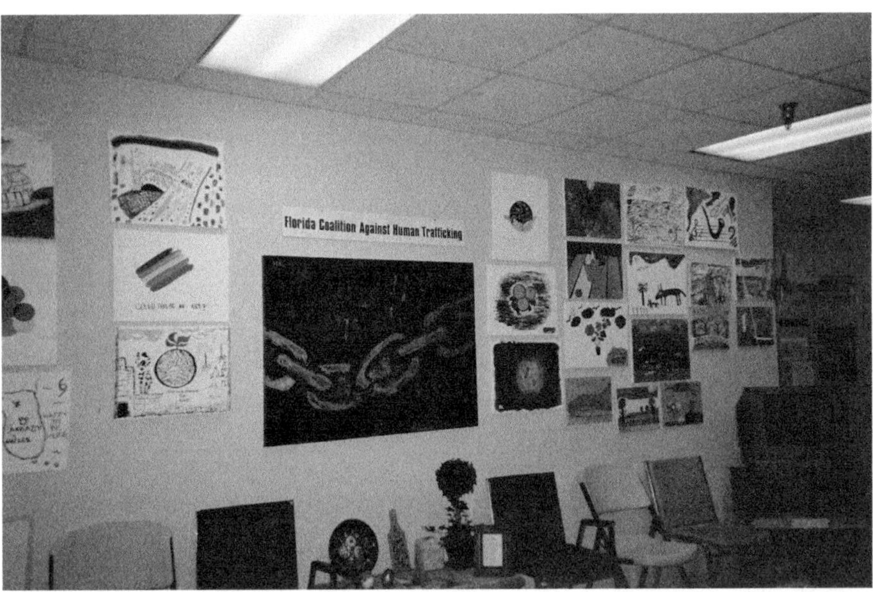

Trafficking survivors' artwork as part of therapy program.

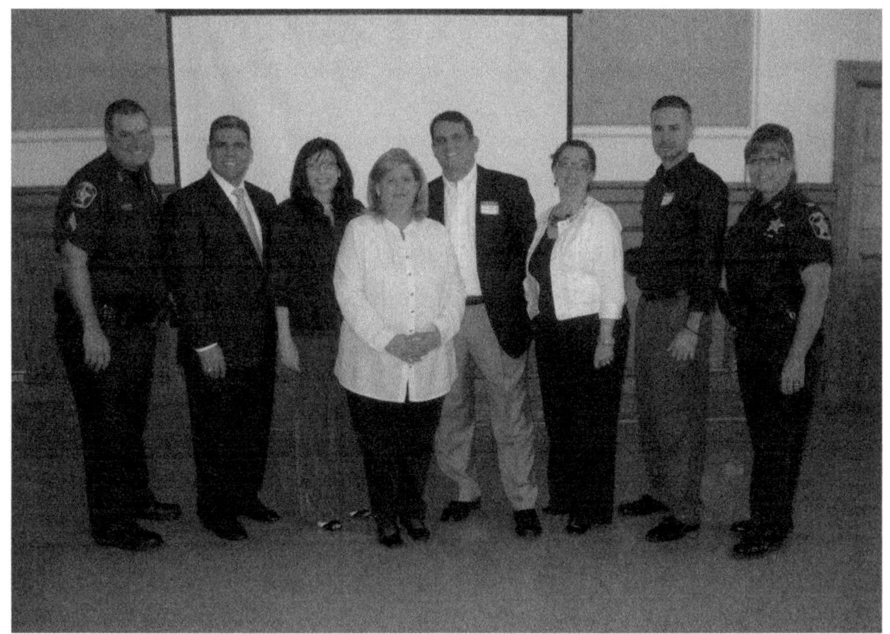

Human Trafficking/Counterfeit Merchandise Training in Polk County. Members of Polk County Sheriff's Office and Hispanic Chamber of Commerce of Polk County.

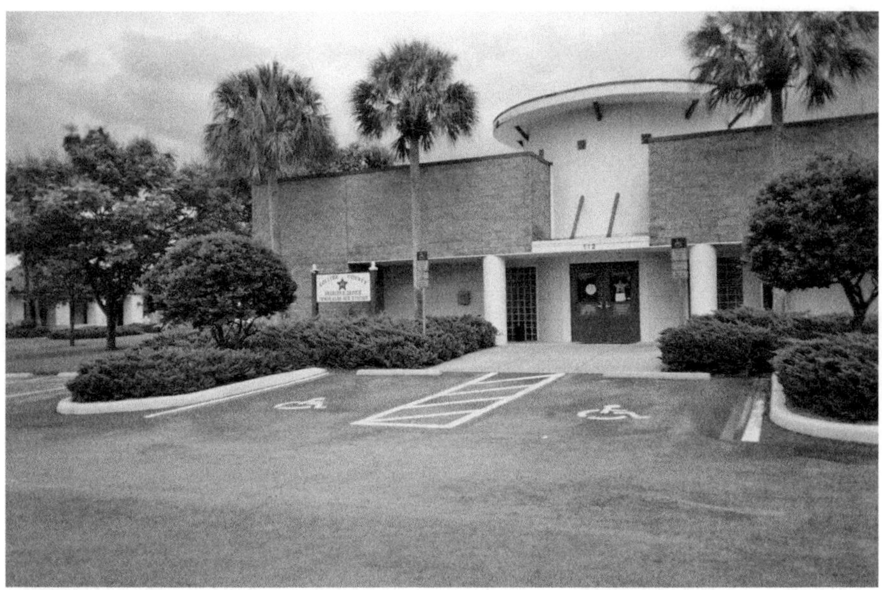

Collier County Sheriff's Office.
Immokalee Substation.

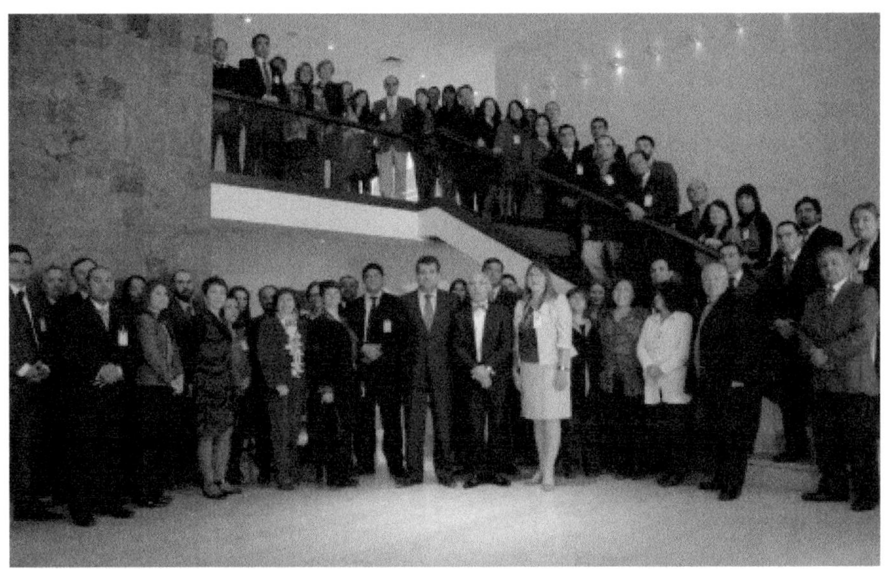

Human Trafficking Training in Chile as
part of Training Delegation with OAS.

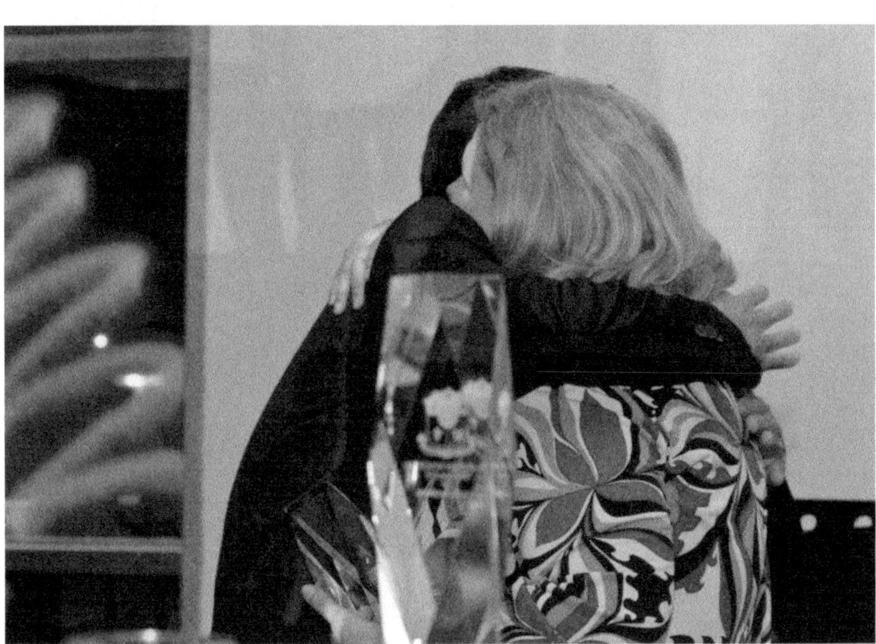

Anna Rodriguez was recognized by BOCA 39 Filipino Case.
Anna being hugged by one of the survivors.

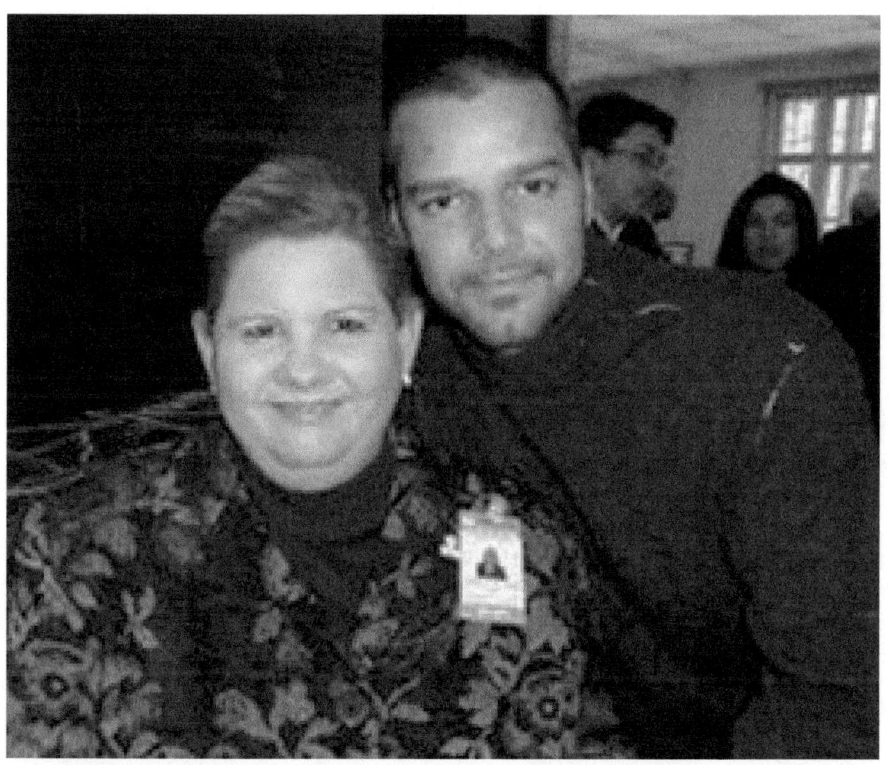

Anna Rodriguez and dear friend, performer, Ricky Martin.
VIP Breakfast in Vienna, Austria UNDOC Human Trafficking Summit.
February 14, 2008.

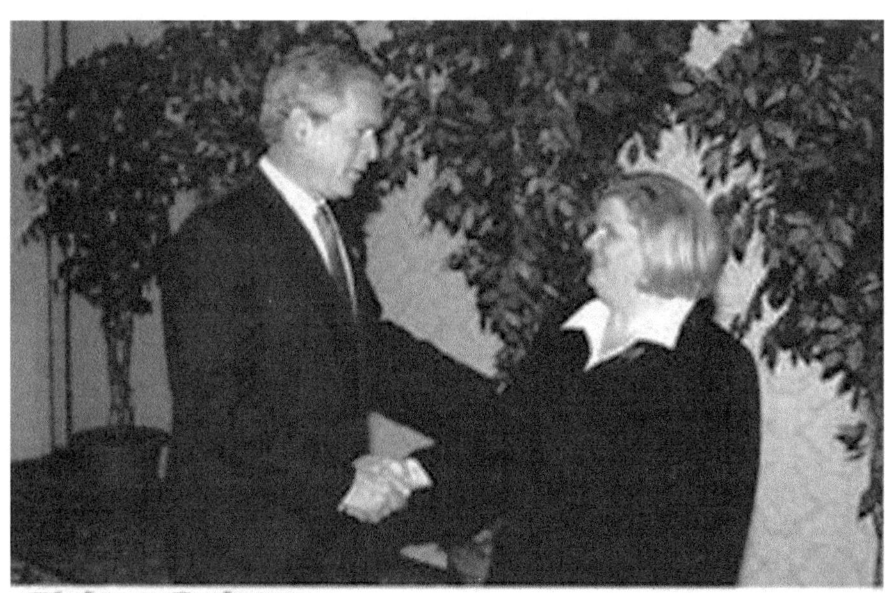

Anna Rodriguez and former US President George W. Bush.
During first National Human Trafficking Conference, Anna was recognized
for her work in the US vs Tecum case. July 16, 2004, Tampa, Florida.